# SUCH A GOOD BABY

RUBY JEAN JENSEN

Gayle J. Foster

# BABY JEREMY HAD ... UNUSUAL POWERS

Someone had touched Felicia. A kind of drawing, tightening fear moved over her body, like the thin trail of a covering of ice, and she instinctively held her own breath, pretending to be asleep. *Someone was in her room, but they were neither moving nor breathing.*

The touch came again, feather-light and death-cold, on both sides of her temples, hands flattened against her skin, palms cupping her, tiny fingertips extended, moving slowly, so slowly down each side of her face to her chin, blindly exploring.

Tiny, tiny hands. Infant hands.

Her eyes opened against her will, and then swept the room in disbelief. For no one was there.

*No one at all.*

First printing: January 1982 in the United States of America

Published by: Gayle J. Foster, Carrollton, Texas

Library of Congress Control Number: 2022906472

Cover art: SelfPubBookCovers.com/ LadyLight

❀ Created with Vellum

*For Theresa*

# CHAPTER 1

This was her punishment, the girl thought as she struggled to take the quick panting breaths the old servant, Celta, told her would make the pain easier to bear. This was her punishment for disobeying her mother ... but why did it keep on and on? The past nine months had laid their own brand of punishment upon her, keeping her isolated from her friends, here in her mother's home, away from school ... and her mother didn't even know what she had done. Her mother thought she had lain with a boy — for how else does a girl get pregnant? — but that wasn't at all what she had done.

*Felicia, don't ever come through the woods at nightfall. It might be dangerous. Keep to the road on your way home from friends' houses. If you forget the time again, call Clint, and have him come after you. He can put your bicycle in the car trunk. Don't stay out after dark! And stay out of the woods at nightfall!*

*Mama, I promise. But I don't know why. There's nothing in the woods ...*

*Felicia!*

*Yes, Mama.*

The pain ... how many hours had it been now? Something ... the baby? ... something was pulling her whole insides out of her, taking with it all of her as it was being born ... *merciful God, where are you?*

There had been other punishments too, increased by her own silence. The echo of her mother's cries of five months ago drifted back, as they so often did, to darken the edges of her consciousness: *She's only a baby herself! How can this be happening to her? Where did she get this — this thing — this pregnancy, when she hasn't even dated a boy? My God in heaven, she's only fourteen years old! Where did this pregnancy come from*?

Her silence had spoken against her. Her bowed head had condemned her. The arguments then between her parents had destroyed her family and had driven her father away, forever, divorced her parents from each other. He had insisted on abortion, Mama had refused.

Let her learn that you can't cover one mistake with another! There will be no abortion for my daughter! We Marchants don't abort our pregnancies!

*Felicia is my daughter too, which makes her name Stewart, not Marchant!*

*Would they, her angry, battling parents, ever have believed that her only mistake had been in disobeying her mother and taking the shortcut through the woods that evening nine months ago? Would anyone, other than Celta, with her old world attitudes, believe*?

Celta stood over her now, wiping her face with a cool, wet washcloth, and her voice was low, heard only by Felicia's sensitive ears. "My Lord, my Lord, save this child from the wrath of the devil, take away the misery — "

The room seemed very dark. Heavy draperies were drawn across the windows, shutting out what light was left of a waning moon. Her bedside lamp was turned off because the light had hurt her eyes, sensitivity increased by her pain. Another lamp, with a low-wattage bulb, burned on the desk, but its pool of light seemed as far beyond her as freedom from this pain. She wanted light, yet shrank from it. She was controlled by the weight in her body that threatened to crush her narrow, slender frame. It was a tumor, huge, gross, heavy, and living. Struggling to survive, fighting her, its prison.

"Mama," she whispered, between breaths. "Where's Mama?"

"She stepped out of the room a minute," Celta bent over her and gently wiped away the moisture that gathered at the corners of her mouth. "She'll be back soon. Quick! Breathe as I told you. It will stop you from tearing so much. This infant can't stay with you forever. It's been much too long now to be in labor for one small lass such as you, much too long for pain to last. Pant and push."

Felicia opened her mouth wider and forced out and sucked in her breath, and blackness swirled closer and closer to her. She reached for it, welcomed it, yet it stayed just beyond her, leaving her in the fire of endless pain ... and her gasps became screams, and her screams returned her in memory to another time when her own pain had turned to screams ... she was coming through the woods, that nightfall last August, nine months ago ...

She had forgotten the time again. There had been so much fun, riding bicycles around the town square, racing with her friends who lived within blocks. Then, pedaling home fast as the sun sank lower in the west and the fat, full moon rose in the east, her bicycle tire struck a sharp little rock and went flat. She stood in the tree-shadowed road with another mile to go, and considered her chances of getting home before dark. There was no way she could call the chauffeur, Clint Reilly, now. No one lived on the road to Tanglewood. Getting home before dark along the road was impossible, but if she took the shortcut through the woods, if she abandoned her bicycle by the side of the road and came back for it tomorrow, no one would ever know. Her mother would not be apt to check up on her until full dark. There was time if she hurried. She knew the way, it was shorter, and she had been there before. There was nothing to be afraid of. Her mother's fear of the forest was silly. What was there to be afraid of? Squirrels? Once over the hill it was only a short way farther into the broad hollow behind Tanglewood, and only a bit more to the brick wall that separated forest from lawns. There was still enough light to find her way, a murky, misty, darkening light, sifted through the trees from both the setting sun and the rising moon. If she hurried, it would be all right.

It was on the top of the hill that she heard the sound.

She paused, listened, concentrated, tried to identify and locate it, for it seemed so close and so strangely ominous. She turned slowly, her eyes searching among the varied deep greens, the lush fullness of heavy foliage and rising dark. Nothing, but the heavy, crowding shadows beneath the drooping leaf-hung tree limbs, the understory shrubbery seeming, now, to be concealing someone who wished to frighten her. And yet, it was not really a voice ... *was it*? It had not been a human sound, had it? It was too piercing, too ultrasonic, so that it was felt more than heard. A vibration, rather than a sound, as though the ground pulsated beneath her feet.

And it was gone, leaving only the cicadas in the trees buzzing merrily, and the katydids sawing their summer songs.

Still, she looked around her, warily, increasingly uneasy, feeling a presence she could not see. She began to move, one cautious step, and as though her movement disturbed it, aroused it to a new alertness the sound rose more audibly, coming now clearly from the ground, continuous, unending.

She whirled, stepping backwards, but the ground foliage, the vines, the vegetation of this summer and eons of summers gone covered and hid whatever lay among it. She dared not move now, to step aside might be to step wrong, and the sound was becoming more vibrant, louder, pitched in different degrees, one above and below another, and was again behind her, and in front of her, and all around her as sound after sound joined in and surrounded her, putting her in its center, encircling, trapping.

Yet she had to escape, to run from this nest of hidden dangers.

*No, my God, no, I don't want to remember this ... this nightmare ... take it away, take this memory ... there is nothing on this earth, in this world, this forest, like this ... take me back to the road, to my bicycle, and let me wake up and find that I am safely on my way home ...*

*Don't touch me ... my God, don't touch me ...*

She was screaming now, her own voice ringing through the woods, stilling the sounds of summer. And mercifully, her memory was taken from her.

Then she was alone, lying among the vines and the leaves, the nightmare moving away into the night.

Another sound rose from the foot of the hill, a loud blare, a car horn, going on and on, stopping abruptly and leaving total silence.

A voice shouted, partway down the hill. "Hey! What's going on up there? Hey! Lady! Are you all right?"

She sat up, her own voice as silent now as death. Dazed, tense with horror, she looked about her, but as before, the foliage of thick summer growth was all she saw. Coming closer up the hillside were footsteps pounding in an awkward run, a man's boots against rocks that broke loose and rolled downward. His voice came again, hesitantly, as though he sensed an inhuman quality in the silence.

"Is somebody there? Does somebody need help?"

She got up, and she ran, on and on toward home, the night air damp on her nakedness for her shorts and panties were left somewhere in the woods. She ran, away from whoever had saved her from… from…

*My God, child, what has happened to you?*

*Celta, please help me. Don't let Mama see me, please. Don't let her see my shirt … don't let her know I've — I've lost my clothes.*

*Come into my room, let me clean you up. My dear Lord, Felicia, who has done this to you? Who has done this thing?*

*I don't know! It — they — weren't human, Celta, do you believe me? I dis-disobeyed Mama and came through the woods, and they — they came up out of the ground, and they — I don't know — I don't — Celta, help me, oh help me! Make me stop bleeding! Mama will think I'm lying, but I'm not, I'm not! My bicycle had a flat — it was closer through the woods, Celta, and I've come that way before, but Mama doesn't know, she must not see me tonight. I don't know what it was — Celta ...*

*Shhh, don't cry, Child. I believe you. I have heard of such things, far back in the old days. I have heard whispers. But oh Lord.*

*Don't let Mama know, Celta. She would never believe ... never …*

*No. No, Child, I will never tell, never. Let me bathe you and put you to bed. Your face shows nothing ... these scrapes on your legs, these raw places, your clothes will cover. I'll tell Mildred that you're not feeling well enough to come down for dinner, but that you got home safe and sound. The bleeding will quit soon. Don't cry, Felicia, it's going to be all right. Surely to God. We will pray that it be all right.*

She slept, and it became only a nightmare, something that she had dreamed, for in the light of day there was only the soreness of her body to remind her, and she needed to believe that it had not really happened.

God had not deserted her.

She had not come through the woods at nightfall.

She was not now giving birth to ... to ...

She was half aware of her bedroom door opening, of silent figures moving toward her bed. But she was not certain that they really existed. That anything other than pain existed. Just before its final thrust, she bent backwards convulsively and screamed, "I want my mama!"

THE YOUNG DOCTOR who had entered this half-lighted room tried not to show his shock. He had been brought out of a deep sleep by a telephone call from a frantic mother who wanted help with her daughter. When he discovered she was from near Jonesboro, he asked her why she hadn't gotten a local doctor, but her answer was too garbled to understand. He had leaned on an elbow in his bed, his eyes still closed, and told the woman to call an ambulance if her daughter needed help so desperately. But her next words woke him up. "My child has been in labor for two days and two nights, doctor, and she's only fourteen years old! I can't take her to a hospital, because I have to protect her from this. Come and help her, please." He sat up even further when he heard the name of the woman's estate: Tanglewood. It belonged to one of the oldest, wealthiest families of Virginia. Scandal had never touched the Marchants of Tanglewood. And now he understood why. The family absorbed its own mistakes and problems as an oyster enclosed and transformed a grain of sand. And so the name of the Marchants remained untainted.

"Turn up the lights," he said now, crisply, "and keep back out of the way. You, there, be prepared to take this infant." He had wondered that the woman thought keeping this child out of a hospital was going to protect her from anything, especially a birth. But it was too late now. The baby was being born.

CONSCIOUSNESS RETURNED GRADUALLY TO FELICIA. It seemed she had been sleeping for a long time, but the figures in the room were clear now, another light had been turned on, and the man standing by the bed was holding a tiny, limp body. Her mother stood beside him, and Celta stood on the other side. All three pairs of eyes were upon the tiny human creature. Felicia saw that it had pale pinkish skin with dark hair on its head, and it had arms and legs like any normal human baby.

Celta began shaking her head portentously. Her thin lips had almost disappeared in their tightness. "Something wrong there," she muttered as she rinsed a washcloth in a pan of water and bent to wipe Felicia's face again. Then she noticed Felicia looking up at the baby.

"Her eyes are open now," Celta said.

The doctor answered without looking at Felicia. "She'll be fine. She's a brave young lady."

"But what's wrong with the child, the baby?" Mildred Marchant Stewart asked, her face pale in the light, almost as pale as her daughter's.

"I'm not sure yet," the doctor said, and turned away toward the desk and its inadequate pool of light beneath a reading lamp. There was a blanket spread there, and he laid the slippery, limp little body on it and began toweling the still arms and legs. His stethoscope indicated a strong heartbeat. But the baby was as still and as limp as though it slept deeply.

Celta had held her peace as long as she could. She mopped the girl's face with increasing vigor. "I'm not surprised. A fourteen-year-old girl is not meant to be a mother. It's too great a burden for her to bear. Her body ain't ready. Nor is her mind."

No one appeared to hear her, not even Felicia, who had turned her face away from the desk. It was good to close her eyes and drift in the blessed comfort of lessened pain. Her mother had gone again to stand at the doctor's side, to look down upon the infant.

"But he's breathing, isn't he?" she asked. Felicia absorbed the fact that her delivered pain had an identity, a sex. It was no longer an it, but a boy. A boy.

"Yes, he's breathing, and he looks absolutely perfect. His heartbeat is as strong as any I've seen, and very regular, even though it is much slower than normal. But there's a lack of response in other ways. I really need to take him to the hospital, Mrs. Stewart. Your daughter is fine, and will be okay right here, but your grandson needs further examination. This birth should have taken place in a hospital. You surely contacted a doctor prior to this?"

"Doctor Fawcett, this is a small community. Our people are very well known here, and have been for generations. To have my daughter confined at the local hospital would have been disastrous for her future. I took her to — out of town — for examinations, and was told there was no reason Felicia should not have a normal delivery. But I had to protect her as much as I could. I don't intend for this to destroy her future, her chances for happiness."

"This is not the Middle Ages, or Victorian — "

"You don't understand," Mildred Marchant Stewart said sharply.

"Then I suggest you let me take the baby for testing. He might have to be institutionalized in any case. It's not uncommon for mothers the age of Felicia to give birth to subnormal children. Female eggs aren't mature at that age, in so many cases. Just as the other lady said, a young girl is not mentally or physically ready, even though she is impregnable. Nature sometimes errs."

"Institutionalized!" Mildred cried. "Of course no Marchant shall ever be institutionalized, Doctor! We can take care of our own. Do what you can for this infant, and then leave us alone."

Celta muttered, "Better let him die, if he will. If the bairn's not normal, then it's probably come to life by way of evil. A changeling. And the changelings, they have terrible powers, they do, and — "

"Shut up, Celta," Mildred said, and came to take the washcloth from her hands. "Go on to your room; I'll tend to Felicia."

The old woman went out, muttering to herself. With shaking hands Mildred took over the bathing of Felicia's face. She brushed the soft hair back, and pulled the blankets up under the smooth, tapered chin. She explained quietly to the doctor, "Celta has been with my family since she was quite a young woman, right out of Ireland. She was my nurse, and Felicia's nurse. But she has never forgotten the old superstitions. To her, an illegitimate child is not just fatherless, but a product of some kind of evil woodland creature, gnomes, or dark fairies or something. She can be surprisingly intolerant even though she is a very good and faithful person. In a way she's still living in the old country, and of course she's getting old now, and senile probably. She has never forgotten her homeland. It's probably time that she be retired and returned."

A soft, clean, fresh blanket was slipped under Felicia's hips, and the blood bathed from her by her mother's hands. Felicia kept her eyes closed. The bed swayed pleasantly beneath her like a hammock blown by the wind. Her mother's touch was gentle and loving. The pain was going away, leaving a tired ache that did not keep her from surrendering to her need for sleep. Her mother's voice was the only sound to reach her.

"I shall rear him as my own, of course," she said. "None of the family shall know anything about the truth of his birth. My divorce from my husband was three months ago, done very quickly and quietly, because we disagreed over an abortion for Felicia. It was a marriage long over anyway, so it didn't matter. He isn't likely to tell anyone the truth, for after all, Felicia is his daughter too. He felt as strongly about this pregnancy as I, and that it should not damage Felicia's future, but he demanded an abortion when he found out about it. At four months he wanted an abortion! I couldn't do that. It would have amounted to murder. But Felicia is my daughter, and her offspring is my responsibility. Therefore, his birth certificate shall read that he was born to me. I'll name him Jeremy."

"Mrs. Stewart, I can't do that."

He had been helping her with the girl part of the time, wondering why she chose to tell him these things. Now he knew. He was to make the deception legal, and once again the Marchant family would have no scandal greater than divorce.

"Of course you can. You will be well paid for your silence about this."

"My silence is assured. There's no need to falsify a birth certificate."

The slender, blond woman straightened and looked at him. Her direct gaze was full of her belief that money bought anything.

"If the birth had been easier, doctor, you wouldn't have been called. And there wouldn't have been a birth certificate at all. If the baby is so subnormal he'll have to be kept at home for his lifetime ... if he's not capable of going into the world — What is it to you, after all? You'd institutionalize him, make him one of many nameless ones? Very few people know of this birth. My ex-husband, myself, you and Celta. I dismissed all the other servants who would have had contact with Felicia in this section of the house. No one else knows."

"You're forgetting the most important."

There was a silence. Then Felicia's mother said, in mild surprise, "Oh, you mean Felicia."

"Yes."

"Felicia is my child. Of course she will not object to my plans for this infant's future. All the Marchants — all my family has grown up here at Tanglewood. I, my brother Martin, Felicia. And now the boy will live here as long as he lives. He will have whatever he needs, whether it's nurses, or, if we're lucky, tutors, and perhaps schools."

"I'm afraid you're not going to be that lucky, Mrs. Stewart. I'd like to examine him more thoroughly, but since he seems physically strong I won't insist on hospitalization. It isn't Down's Syndrome. He's a very beautiful infant. There's a chance he may come out of it, kicking and yelling, but right now he seems to be deeply asleep. Almost in hibernation. With your permission I'll look in on him, and your daughter, for a few days at least."

"I'll call you again if I need you, Dr. Fawcett. If you're not willing to alter a birth certificate, to make life easier on these two children, then I'm sure you have done all you can for us."

"At this early stage, if there's a physical abnormality, the infant might be helped. As I said, he seems fine, physically, in most ways. But I should think you'd want to know for sure."

"Whatever his capabilities," Felicia's mother was saying, drifting farther and farther away as Felicia slid softly toward sleep, "he will be safe here at Tanglewood."

In the south wing, adjoining Mildred's suite of rooms, the old nursery had been readied for the expected baby. As soon as Mildred had bathed and dressed the baby, he was taken there, and Celta summoned to stay with him. In a few more days a nurse would be coming, already hired and waiting in a city several hundred miles away. Mildred had gone to extensive lengths to make sure no one would suspect this child to be anyone's but her own. The need for secrecy was so deeply ingrained in her by her rigid upbringing that she found it easier to bend to its will than to defy it. The child, Jeremy, was hers. Baby brother of the beautiful young daughter who had now passed her fourteenth birthday. Old friends and acquaintances would say to her, when they knew: "How delightful to have a baby again, with your daughter growing up." But of course they wouldn't mean it, for what woman in her late thirties wanted that business again? Now, however, if the baby actually was subnormal to the point of retardation, he would have to remain a permanent secret, kept to his own part of the house, his own backyard.

THE HOUSE WAS QUIET NOW, the sun rising and turning the lamps a sickly yellow. The west wing, in which Felicia had been safely ensconced for the last three months, was as silent as a tomb. The sun would not reach this section of the house until late in the day, protected as it was by tall evergreens on the south, and the higher rise of the central portion of the house. Felicia was alone in the west wing, in the room on the southwest corner where the light was most generous. She hadn't objected to the move from her old room. In those days she hadn't objected to anything. For a while, in fact for many months, it had looked as though the pregnancy was draining her of all life, leaving only her large eyes to observe dully a distant future, the distant horizon, or nothing. For the past several months she had been only slightly more responsive than her baby was now.

Mildred left Felicia's room, closing the door softly. Let the girl sleep. Perhaps the rest would help bring her back to normal, to that vivacious, bright-eyed girl of last year.

To her surprise, Mildred found that Celta was waiting in the hall outside Felicia's room.

"You haven't left the baby in the nursery alone, have you, Celta?" Mildred asked, her tone clearly expressing criticism.

"Ma'am" Celta said formally, as she did only on those rare occasions when she had something very important to say, "I must talk to you where the lass cannot hear us."

Mildred walked along the hall briskly, allowing Celta to keep up as she could.

"Must we talk now, Celta? I'm very tired. The past few days and nights have been an exhausting trial, as you well know."

Celta kept up, her long-legged stride graceless and awkward. "Ma'am, I don't feel it can wait. It's about the bairn, Ma'am."

Mildred sighed. "Yes, of course. Hurry with it and get back to him."

"I'm begging you, Ma'am, to listen to the doctor, and let him take this bairn away and put it in an institution. For her sake as well as his."

"For goodness sake, why, Celta? His nursery is over in the wing by my rooms, not hers. He'll not upset her."

"The thing is, Ma'am, you don't know where it came from, this bairn. You don't know whose blood runs in his veins. You don't — "

Mildred stopped abruptly and faced Celta. "Do you know something you haven't told me, Celta?"

Celta's eyes did not waver. Her only sign of nervousness was the increased tightness of her thin lips. "No, Ma'am, I don't know who the father is."

Mildred stared at Celta a moment longer. She began walking on, more slowly now.

"Ma'am, it's better that you listen to the doctor. There are some things in this world that we ought not to tamper with. This bairn — I have a feeling — he's one of them."

"Celta, I think you should go to bed in the room beside the nursery. Just leave the door open as you always did with Felicia, so that you can hear him if he wakes and cries. He'll probably be ready for a feeding by the time you get back to him."

"Ma'am — "

"Obviously, you too are exhausted. How many nights has it been since you slept for more than ten minutes? When you wake you'll feel better about everything. And now, Celta, goodnight. I don't want to discuss this anymore. You won't have to look after him very long. The nurse should be here in a few days."

Celta paused, and watched Mildred Marchant Stewart go on down the hall and turn the corner toward the central part of the house. Then, slowly, she followed, going reluctantly toward the nursery.

The touch on Felicia's face woke her, and at first she was disoriented. The heavy draperies were drawn, the lights turned off, the room without sound. She sensed her aloneness ... and yet she was not alone, for someone had touched her. But they were being very, very still, and scarcely breathing at all, for she heard nothing; and a kind of drawing, tightening fear moved over her body, like the thin trail of a covering of ice. She instinctively held her own breath, pretending to be asleep, while her senses sharpened, her ears picking up the sounds of her own body, and nothing more. *Someone was in her room, but they were neither moving nor breathing.*

The touch came again, feather-light and death-cold, on both sides of her temples, hands flattened against her skin, palms cupping her, tiny fingertips extended, moving slowly, so slowly down each side of her face to her chin, blindly exploring. Tiny, tiny hands. Infant hands.

The fear that gripped her immobilized her legs, pinned her arms to the bed and stilled her voice. Her eyes opened against her will, and then swept the room in disbelief. For no one was there.

No one at all.

## CHAPTER 2

The baby Jeremy opened his eyes for the first time on the tenth day of his life. Celta had just bathed and dressed him in a soft, warm gown, diaper and band, wrapped him in a blanket and sat down to rock him. He took the bottle eagerly, as he had from the beginning, a pink, greedy little mouth with mild edging from the corners. He was soft and warm and pliable in her arms, yet Celta wished the nurse would come on and get there and take the infant off her hands, for she had known about changelings all her life, and couldn't help but feel uncomfortable around this strange bairn. She didn't look down into his face more often than she could help, and would have stuck him into his cradle and propped the bottle up to his mouth with a small pillow but for her mistress's objections. "Hold him when you feed him," Mildred had ordered. And so Celta held him and fed him his bottle, wishing all the time the nurse would hurry and arrive and spare her the job.

She felt the pull of his eyes. She didn't want to look down into his face and meet them straight on, but she couldn't help herself. They were staring up at her, and she felt herself recoil from the deep smoky blueness she saw there. As though he knew what she was thinking and feeling, he stared at her while his round little cheeks worked at the nipple and milk formed in drops at the corners of his small mouth. Then, for the first time in her years of service, Celta disobeyed her mistress. She held the baby away from her, arm's length, and carried him to the cradle. While the eyes stared upwards, following her face, never wavering or blinking, she lay him in the cradle and propped the bottle beside his face. When she hurried from the room he made his first sound. It was only a whimper, as though he hadn't yet learned how to cry.

Celta closed the door hastily, leaving him alone.

She didn't tell her mistress what she had seen and heard.

THE NURSE ARRIVED THAT MORNING, depositing her luggage on the steps of Tanglewood while the taxi that had brought her from the small local airport continued on around the circle drive and back to town. She was a widow in her fifties, a practical nurse who had tired of hospital work. Her face was round and made up only by a touch of lipstick. She had been moderately pretty as a girl, with no great ambitions. Her life had turned out much as she had planned, with husband and four children, except the husband was gone too early from her life. But that was two years ago, and her grief was hidden behind the veil of time, no longer a source of pain. This was her first job as a private nurse, and it sounded ideal. Her children didn't need her any more except as a babysitter and, she had decided with fervor, if she was going to spend her evenings babysitting, she might as well be paid for it, and well paid.

The house was intimidating, but interesting. She had been on the outside of houses like this all her life — like most people — and for the first time she was going in. She rang the doorbell, and heard musical chimes beyond the walls, faintly.

She waited.

Somewhere beyond the hedges and brick garden walls she heard a scream. At first the sound crawled over her skin as if every tiny hair had turned alive and moving, but then she laughed at herself. A memory, far back in her childhood, swept forward to save her. The call of a peacock, that was what it was. Not a scream, but a cry, a song, so to speak. She listened, and a moment later it came again. She could almost see him strut his feathers before his hens.

She pressed the doorbell again and turned her back to the door to look at the circle drive, the round lawn and flower beds in the center, the tall trees that so neatly followed the edge of the paved driveway, the blacktopped road beyond and the drop into the valley and tree-banked river. No wonder these people could afford to pay $1,800 a month for a full-time nurse. The doctor she had worked for off and on over the years had called her about it, and even though it was four hundred miles from her own home, she had grabbed it. With reservations. For it had sounded too good to be true.

They'd had a conversation about it: "Why didn't they get a local nurse?" she had asked. "There has to be a catch of some kind."

The doctor had rubbed his white mustache and pinched his chin, both unconscious habits that indicated puzzlement. "That's what I thought, too, but everything seems to be on the up and up. The attorney who contacted me about it is an old friend. We went to school together. That's a small community. That is, it's more rural than this; so I suppose a good nurse was not easily found. They probably all have jobs there already, and staying with an infant twenty-four hours a day is not exactly the most exciting thing in the world."

"There's no special medical problem?"

"Uh ... I asked that, and was told nothing difficult to handle. If you don't feel you want to take any chances — "

"Oh, I'll take the job, Doctor," she had said hurriedly. "How long will they be wanting a private nurse?" At that much money, she was thinking, plus room and board, in a year's time she would have a bank account of over twenty thousand, for her personal needs were small. And twenty thousand would go a long way in assuring her a comfortable old age. Of course she would take the job, even if there were special problems of a severe nature. Obviously he could be kept at home, or he would be in a special hospital.

"Indefinitely," he had said. "There was no mention of time, so it might be one month, or two years or more."

One month? That might account for the pay. "I'll take it anyway," she had said. With round-trip expenses paid, she couldn't lose. And now she was here.

She heard no footstep; the wide door opened with only a soft sliding movement. Janet Duncan swung back with a smile on her face. Just inside the shadowed house an elderly gray-haired woman peeped out, and then, on seeing the luggage, her weathered face eased into a smile and she opened the door wider.

"Might you be the nurse?"

"I'm Janet Duncan," Janet said, keeping a smile on her face. "I've come to — "

"Yes." The woman was tall and thin and slightly stooped, but her skinny arms were strong and tough as leather. She grabbed a suitcase in each hand. "Come on in, Miss Duncan. We've been waiting for you. How on earth did you get here?"

"A taxi from the — "

"Oh. Well, I don't know why Clint — that's the chauffeur — didn't pick you up. Come on, come on, Miss."

It was obvious the maid would not allow her to finish a sentence, so Janet stopped bothering to try. She merely smiled, and supplied the missing word. "Janet."

"We've been expecting you for a couple of days now, but thought you'd call from the airport or wherever you came from. The mistress might want to see you first, I expect, but she didn't give me any orders about it, so she'll know where to find you."

Janet took the only piece of luggage left, a small overnight case, and followed into the hall. She looked around swiftly and with amazement. It could be called a hall, so far as her experience went, only because it was attached to the front entry door and had a stairway rising from its depths. As far as size went, it could have swallowed her three-room apartment with no effort. There was a huge grandfather clock, a settee and matching chairs that would have brought a fortune at an antique auction, and other large, dark pieces of furniture that, she promised herself, she would take a look at later, for they all looked as though they had been sitting in the same places for at least a hundred and fifty years. The atmosphere was almost tomblike, though, bearing upon the still, chill air the suggestion of lowered voices of long ago.

"I'm Celta," the maid said, her thin arms lifting the heavy suitcases clear of the bottom step of the rising stairway, elbows bent outward sharply. "Come on up and I'll show you your rooms."

"Let me carry those, Celta."

"I've got them. Just come along. The bairn will need feeding again soon, and I don't want the job. The mistress will see you later, I'm sure. She'd want me to show you where to put your things. And show the bairn to you."

Janet followed the spidery legs up the long, graceful stairway and along the balcony to a front suite of rooms. The balcony was edged by fluted columns and banisters and so thickly and deeply carpeted that every footfall was rendered utterly silent. The bedroom into which Celta dumped the suitcases was also carpeted as lushly as the upstairs balcony. The colors here were light and dark blue, and a southern window, which would let in plenty of winter sunshine, was now open to the mild spring breeze that wafted in from the tall trees and valley-nestled river. Celta scarcely paused after ridding herself of the luggage. She pounced upon a closed door, opened it with a jerk, and then stepped back, her job finished. She did not even look into the adjoining room.

"There is the nursery," she said. "And beyond the nursery is the hallway to Mrs. Stewart's rooms. If you need her, all you do is go along the hallway the other side of the nursery and knock on her door. But don't bother her if you don't have to. The bairn, he'll give you no trouble, no trouble at all."

"I'd like to see him now," Janet said, expecting Celta to lead the way into the nursery. But Celta moved instead toward the doorway through which they had entered.

"Just go ahead, you'll find everything you need either in the nursery or in the bathroom. My job is down in the kitchen right now. Other help has been hired and is expected, but until they come I'll be working downstairs."

The grandfather clock began striking the hour of eleven, and the slow, deep, penetrating tones drifted upward and diffused through the upper story. It was the only sound in the house at that moment. Celta closed the bedroom door, and the clock's voice became muffled and far away. Janet smiled and shrugged. Celta no doubt was an odd old girl with a dislike for doing anything other than the chores she considered her own.

The nursery was the kind most young mothers dream of: bright, light, sunshiny, cool, sheer priscilla curtains moving in the breeze, double windows facing south. In the tree branch outside the windows a cardinal sang, its voice as bright and as beautiful as its coat of red. The wallpaper was nursery rhyme stuff, and the furniture was painted yellow with nursery rhyme figures. There was a crib, but it was empty. Near the windows was a cradle with hood of white wicker draped with blue netting and white satin. Janet went over and looked in, expecting she knew not what, but slightly tensed, as though to brace herself for deformity of an atrocious kind, or, to let her imagination go wild, horns or something of that nature.

She stared. The infant was no more than a week or two old and lay sleeping, with tiny, closed fists against its cheeks. The head was perfect, round, small, beautiful. The hair was dark, as were the winged, little eyebrows and long eyelashes. She had never seen a baby more beautiful than this, but the blanket was drawn up to its chin. The deformity must be hidden, if there was a deformity. Just exactly why she had drawn that opinion she was not sure, but there were subtle warnings, it seemed to her, such as hiring a nurse from so far away, and such as Celta's behavior — as though she couldn't wait to get out of the room next to the nursery.

To avoid waking the baby, Janet eased the blanket back ever so slowly, even though her experience with babies assured her they were not easily awakened if they slept soundly. Most of them put up with being rolled about and dressed or undressed quite well without awakening.

He was dressed in diaper and gown, and his legs and feet, the lower part of his body, were as perfect as the upper. Faintly puzzled, she tucked the blanket in again, noting with half a mind the softness of it, the obvious richness. It had to be cashmere. Nothing else would be so soft. She noticed suddenly, and with a start, that the baby's eyes had opened. He was looking up at her through inky blue depths, with an intensity that seemed far, far beyond his age. She was nonplussed for only a moment, and then his total being became the stronger force. He was a tiny, helpless baby, and her imagination had been running away with her for several days now, she realized. She began crooning, an automatic response to little fellows this age and size, and slipped her hands under his body, one hand cupping his head, the other his narrow little rear. She brought him up, blanket and all, and put him against her shoulder.

"Ah him's a lovely little baby boy, yes, him is — "

Her chin was turned, lightly touching his forehead where he lay on her shoulder. She felt no movement of his body, no warning lurch no matter how subtle. Suddenly copious vomit was there, spewing out onto her neck, running down the front of her dress, a slimy, reeking rotted liquid such as she had never seen.

"My God," she cried softly under her breath, and held him just slightly away from her. The vomiting had stopped, and he gazed at her blandly, his small mouth closed, his chin dry and clean with not so much as a drop clinging.

"Oh! What a mess. Did he cough up on you?" A woman had just entered the nursery from the small hallway on the far side.

Janet held the baby out away from her dress and looked up. The woman who stood there looking so delicate and helpless was without a doubt Mrs. Stewart. She was slender and expensive-looking, wearing a long, flowing silk caftan. Her hair was brightly blond and well coiffured. She was medium-sized. She looked around thirty or thirty-five years old, although Janet knew that age would be hard to tell on this lady. She was too well cared for, too carefully bleached and set and combed. Janet smiled her ever-ready smile.

"A bit," she said. "But he didn't get a drop on himself. It won't take me long to clean up."

"Fine." Mrs. Stewart had an ever-ready smile of her own, and it was as carefully unrevealing as Janet's. "You go ahead and change. I'll stay with him until you get back." The woman made no move to take the baby, so Janet put him in the cradle again.

In her room Janet found a private bath, and within minutes had removed her soiled dress and replaced it with a clean one. The dress stank revoltingly, but she didn't have time to handle it properly. She ran the wash basin full of water and submerged the dress. She washed and dried her hands and hurried back to the nursery. The smell came with her, trailing in the still air, not to be escaped.

Mrs. Stewart was standing by the windows looking out. The cradle sat very still. The baby obviously was not moving at all, Janet noted without looking inside. With no further delay she introduced herself and added a few explanations: "I was brought right on upstairs by Celta just a few minutes ago. I didn't get a chance to ask her any particulars about the baby — his name, or anything like that — or whether there are special instructions."

"I'm the one you'll come to when you need help, Mrs. Duncan. I'm Mildred Stewart, the baby's mother, and my rooms are just through the adjoining hall opposite the door to your room. Don't you need some time to unpack and get settled? I'm sure Celta can continue to take care of the baby for a few hours. Until you've had time to get acquainted with your surroundings."

"No, that's all right. I don't mind taking over right away. I can unpack when the baby's sleeping. At his age, they sleep a lot. But, I need to know of any medical problems he has — "

"No medical problems," Mildred Stewart said quickly. "He usually doesn't even spit up his milk. I can't imagine why he did that."

Janet went to the cradle and looked down. He was asleep again.

"It's nothing to be alarmed about, if it doesn't happen too much," Janet said, but her eyebrows drew closer together. She felt a vague unease. The arms and legs were too still, she felt. His vomit had been too voluminous and too putrid. "His checkup was all right, I assume?"

"Yes, of course, he's fine. You asked about his name — it's Jeremy, and he was a week old Tuesday." She directed an impersonal smile at Janet as she moved toward the hallway to her rooms. "All you need is right here, but of course you'll be going down to the kitchen for milk and other things, and you can either take your meals with the family or in your own room, whichever you prefer. The kitchen is down the front stairway and back through the double doors at the rear of the hall, or go to the back hall here on this floor, where you'll find the service stairway down to the kitchen area. You are in the central portion of the house here, sometimes called the south wing. You probably noticed there are east and west wings also, but they need not concern you in the least except for general looking about. The west wing is occupied only by my daughter. The east wing houses the servants as well as guests. But at the moment there are no guests, and no live-in servants. Of course Celta lives here, but her apartment is down by the kitchen. If there's anything else, Mrs. Duncan, you can feel free to call on me."

Even as she talked she was moving away, edging toward her own rooms. Janet watched her in amazement. The baby's mother hadn't so much as looked in on him, had shown no affection for him, had made no move to touch him that she saw. Was this the way the child had been treated since he was born? It was no wonder he didn't move about much.

She looked around and found a small refrigerator with several bottles of formula already mixed. There were six more cans of milk. On a small cabinet beside the refrigerator was a bottle warmer. A small sterilizing machine held clean bottles. There was also a small wicker basket of oranges, an electric juicer, a strainer. There were towels and washcloths and soaps and lotions and chests of baby clothes. Just as Mrs. Stewart had said, as Celta had said, there was everything she needed. Everything a baby needed ... except love? But of course she was jumping to a conclusion. Just because Celta showed an impatience to get away from the nursery, and just as the baby's mother had shown a similar impatience, didn't really add up to no love. Janet cautioned herself to be careful about forming opinions. There might be a lot here that she hadn't seen yet.

The first few hours passed uneventfully. Baby Jeremy slept, and Janet washed out her dress and hung it to dry over her bathtub. The odor still lingered; she took it downstairs to the kitchen, where she found Celta. Celta showed her the laundry room and Janet tossed the dress into the washing machine and ran it fifteen minutes. While she was there she ate her lunch and looked about the back yard, finding terraces and gardens and fountains, lovely, private places to sit, and to walk, and to push the baby's buggy.

She returned to the nursery to find the baby awake, his unmoving gaze directed upward toward a ceiling he surely couldn't see. His hands lay against his cheeks, just as they had when she first looked at him, and his legs were drawn up slightly. It occurred to her that he might not have been very thoroughly tested medically, and might even be blind and paralyzed. A feeling of sympathy moved into her heart at that thought. She had taken for granted that Mrs. Stewart was right when she said the baby was fine — but was he?

Janet bent over the cradle. The baby's eyes shifted just slightly, its gaze moving from the faraway ceiling to her face. But, Janet wondered, was he really seeing? She put her hand above his face, but the eyes didn't blink, they merely closed. She drew her hand away, and the eyes opened again. He stared directly at her, looking into her eyes, and she felt a contest of wills, as though he knew she was testing him in a way, experimenting with him. She drew back a bit, and then smiled at her foolishness. Still testing, she moved her hand over his eyes again, and again he closed them.

So, he could see, after all. But could he move?

She slid her finger into his tiny fist, but it did not tighten on hers. The eyes were open again, and watching her.

She opened his fist, straightening the bent fingers, and they pulled suddenly against her, closing upon her, their thin, sharp little nails raking into her flesh with fiery cuts. She gasped and drew her hand away. Tiny flecks of blood appeared along the scratches. The pain was like the pain of a paper cut, burning and far greater than she anticipated. But at least she had discovered that he could move if he wished to. She spread his hands again, looking at the uncut nails.

They had grown so long they curled, like colorless, transparent claws. Janet grunted in disapproval and dug from the top drawer of the chest small, new, silver nail clippers that most obviously had never been used. Didn't Celta know how to take care of a baby? Didn't the baby's mother know to check on such things as sharp little fingernails? It was a wonder the boy hadn't scratched his face to a bloody pulp. His lack of movement had probably saved him. With his tiny hands forced open she clipped the nails closely to the miniscule fingertips.

"There now," she said, "there'll be no more scratching. As soon as I put some iodine on my hand, we'll see about some supper. I know for certain that you haven't eaten a bite in four hours, for I've been here that long myself. Don't you ever cry, Jeremy? Don't you ever ask for anything?"

Janet put a bottle of formula into the bottle warmer and turned back to take the baby up from the cradle. She slipped her hands under him and stopped, her heart beginning a long, slow pound of warning, for the baby's eyes were blank and glazed and staring at nothing, his arms and legs thrown back limply. *He is dead.* In the moment she had turned away, what little life there was in his body had fled, leaving him forever unmoving and unasking.

Janet jerked him up, a limp doll with hanging arms and legs and lolling head. She shook him. She lay him on the cabinet top and bent over him, her ear pressed to his narrow chest. It was only a flutter, it seemed, but it was there, faintly. His heart was beating after all. He wasn't dead ... he hadn't died ... he had only had a spell of some kind ... was still having a spell ...

She took him into her arms, the blanket tossed away. She held him cradled against her heart, and looked around the room for a telephone. When she found it, she jerked it up, seeing there was no dial, only a couple of buttons indicating an in-house line. She pressed one of the buttons and heard a ring somewhere along the line. They hadn't told her what to do in an emergency such as this ... they hadn't told her ...

"Yes?" Celta's voice said irritably.

"I need a line to a doctor," Janet said quickly, trying to speak coherently. "Something is wrong with the baby. Please get his doctor immediately."

"Is he limp and kind of lifeless?" Celta asked without hurry.

"Yes! Would you please — "

"He'll be all right," Celta said. "He does that sometimes, that's all. He'll come around." The phone clicked and Janet was left holding a useless receiver. She dropped it, and it dangled, swinging, from its short cord.

Mrs. Stewart, she thought now. But of course! She should not have tried to call a doctor on her own. With the nearly lifeless infant in her arms she ran into the narrow hall and to the closed door at its ends. She knocked frantically, calling, "Mrs. Stewart!"

• • •

FELICIA LAY crossways on her bed, her arm her pillow. She stared pensively at the closed draperies. On the bedside table a small portable radio played softly, a background for her thoughts. She had gotten up and dressed this morning, in the first thing she had pulled out of the closet — a dress with an elastic waist — but after that she had lain down again. It was the first time she had worn anything other than babydoll pajamas or robes since the birth of the baby.

She couldn't get her mind off him. Everything she looked at reminded her. She had closed the draperies again. When she opened them, the first thing she saw was the forest stretching back of the house toward the hills, rising against the sky, covered with the deep, rich green of summer. She loved the forest, and yet now she was frightened of it. When she looked at it she was reminded of that nightmare ... the one she tried so often to forget, or to remember completely.

But she didn't want to think about it.

She turned over onto her back, and the soft music became the background for another sound, one that stiffened her body in a strange dread. The dread was, in a way, more frightening than any she had ever known, for it was edged by anticipation. It was a sound softer than the music, yet in some way more pronounced, and might have been anywhere — in the walls, or the ceiling, or along the panels of her closed door. A movement, a gliding of a formless body, or a hand, along smooth wood.

*The slither of a snake along the floor.*

*No!*

She sat up, her breath suspended, and waited. And when it was gone, as though it had come as far as it could, she knew that nothing more would come today, for there was something about the light that held him away from her. When the darkness came, when the house slept, he came nearer, and the touch was cold, so cold. Waking her, always. Making her heart pound in terror.

*What did he want with her?*

For she sensed he was searching for her — especially for her. Did he know that she was his mother? And that she was, in some way, still connected to him?

She wondered what he looked like. She had seen him only once, and that on the night of his birth. She had heard them say he was physically perfect and possibly mentally subnormal.

Something was wrong with him.

How could he reach her, through the walls, through space, and lay his tiny hands on her? Or was this, too, only an extension of the nightmare! Perhaps he really didn't exist at all. Perhaps, on that day, riding home on her bicycle, she had fallen and struck her head, and no longer was able to see the world as others saw it.

Perhaps she had really gone insane, and none of this was real.

She dared not ask her mother, nor even Celta. She had to try to understand for herself exactly what had happened. Or try harder to forget, and live in this new world that had become twisted and strange and filled with fears.

The only sound in her room now was the radio. He was gone. Whatever he was, he was gone.

Felicia turned off her radio and went to the window, deliberately opened the drapes and looked out. To the south below was the gentle slope of the valley, the level stretch of pasture-land, and the tree-lined river.

To the northwest and north was the forest.

She sat down on the windowsill, looking at the trees, the dark green of tall pines among the paler green of oaks, maples, sycamores. For a long while she stared at the forest, remembering the squirrels who lived there, and the other little animals, and the initials (hers) she had carved on the big sycamore tree by the spring, until at last her pulse slowed and the fear lay dormant.

Only the curiosity remained.

Did the baby, whom her mother had named Jeremy, really exist?

And if he did, who was he, and what did he want of her?

Did he know that even in their separation she had felt increasingly drawn to him?

THERE WAS no answer to Janet's calls, and after a while she turned indecisively away from the door to Mrs. Stewart's suite. She became suddenly aware that the lifeless body in her arms had stretched backwards, as though in preparation now for a convulsion. She would know how to handle that. But then he drew a long sigh and his body relaxed and curled, becoming smaller, more complaint; his arms drew up against his chest and his hands folded into the tiny fists that pressed against his cheeks. His legs relaxed, drew up, and he was once again a normal, sleeping infant. Janet looked down at him, her heart slowing until she felt weak with relief. She returned to the nursery and prepared to lay the sleeping infant back into his cradle; but someone had entered the room, was standing just inside the nursery door. Janet's overexcited heart leaped into alarm again ... but she saw it was only a girl.

At first glance the girl was a specter, a silent ghost with long straight hair and a still face, pale and set. She stood unmoving, silent, as though she were in strange territory and dared not take a step farther into the room. But then Janet saw the eyes, large, dark and alive. They were looking intently at the sleeping baby.

"Hello," Janet said, the baby warm in her arms. The girl didn't answer, and Janet followed her eyes and looked down. The infant was oddly beautiful, a smile dimpling, appearing and disappearing; now so completely normal. But Janet felt a sudden need to put him down and move away, a primitive urge to run. She hurried to the cradle and put him in.

The girl spoke softly: "Who are you?"

Janet drew a long breath. It was the plane flight, it had to be. Why else would she react as she had, almost going into shock over such little things as a baby going limp, as a girl coming unexpectedly into the room? "I'm Janet Duncan, the new nurse. I arrived this morning."

But the girl's attention seemed pinpointed on the cradle and its occupant, as though she had forgotten she had even asked a question, and certainly as though the answer to that question was unimportant. Janet looked at her more closely, saw a girl of perhaps fourteen or fifteen, with unusually pretty features, delicately molded and vividly colored even though she seemed now to be pale. Her lips were pink and rich, but untouched with rouge. There was a resemblance to the infant, Janet saw, even though the baby's features were not clearly formed yet. The eyebrows were the same, and the long lashes. The girl was quite tall, with a slender, narrow frame; so would the boy be when he grew up.

Janet said, "You must be baby Jeremy's sister." The girl's eyes widened and flew instantly to meet her own. Janet met the stare in silence. The answer was long in coming and almost a whisper. "Yes."

Janet forced her professional smile. She longed to be home, home where she could get away from her work, home where her own noisy grandchildren did not give her this odd, uneasy, shivery feeling. She said now, "You look like him."

The girl said, "You may go now, if you'd like. I'll stay with the baby for a while. I don't mind staying an hour — or longer."

Janet felt she should say no. She hadn't been given such instructions by her employer; but she could not. She needed to get out, to take a walk through the gardens and into the woods beyond the back of the house. She nodded acquiescence.

At the door she looked back and saw the girl bending over the cradle, her long hair falling forward and almost totally concealing her face.

But the smile, so gentle and tender, was not hidden.

It was not the smile of an older sister.

# CHAPTER 3

Felicia crooned under her breath, words meant only for baby Jeremy:

"I'm here, my precious. I've come to you."

She slipped her hands beneath him and lifted him, and saw that he was beautiful. She held him against her breast, with his downy little head tucked between her cheek and her shoulder. He was so tiny, so warm, so sweet-smelling with the talcum powders and the milk breath. He opened his eyes and looked at her, and she saw an intelligence in the blue, blue depths. He was, after all, far more special than any other child ever born, was he not? And he wanted her. He had wanted her so desperately, and had called and beckoned to her in his strange way that at first had frightened her almost to cold shock. It had taken days and nights before she could accept knowing whose hands touched her ...

All the walls, all the walls within walls, could not keep him from her. And now at last she had come to him.

She held his hand and counted his fingers, and felt the warm moistness of his palm. Warm. Warm and alive and real.

Oh, he was so very real!

She took him now to the rocking chair by the windows, and sat down with him and began rocking gently and crooning softly, words that meant something, words that meant nothing. His narrow, diapered little bottom fit into the palm of her hand, and the back of his head nestled into the other, and Felicia recited a favorite old nursery rhyme softly:

"WYNKEN, Blynken and Nod, one night,
  Sailed off in a wooden shoe.
  Sailed on a river of misty light
  Into a sea of dew ..."

SHE FELT HIM LISTENING, scarcely breathing, contented now against the beat of her heart, the gentle rise and fall of her breast as she breathed ...

"WHERE ARE you going and what do you wish?
  The old moon asked the three.
  We have come to fish for the herring fish
  That live in this beautiful sea;
  Nets of silver and gold have we ...
  Said Wynken, Blynken and Nod ..."

DOWNSTAIRS, Janet searched the branching hallways for an exit door, hoping to avoid seeing anyone, but she couldn't have made a worse choice. She went out onto a terrace — just a narrow strip of grass from the beginning of the forest and the rise of the hill at the northeast corner of the house — and found herself face to face with her employer, Mildred Stewart. This lady of the artificially bright hair and long manicured fingernails was wearing an old shirt over jeans, gardening gloves, and a straw hat decorated with plastic berries. They both stopped short, surprised. Mrs. Stewart spoke, the meaningless smile already in place.

"Oh, Mrs. Duncan. Are you out for a stroll?"

Janet felt sure she had almost said *another stroll,* and answered guiltily, "I thought I — yes, I guess you could say I am. But I didn't leave the baby alone, Ma'am. A young girl — your daughter, I assume — is with him."

Mildred Stewart's smile disappeared. "Felicia?" Her tone of voice hadn't altered, but it was with an obvious inner struggle that she brought back the smile, the mask she would no doubt use with all employees. "Felicia is babysitting!"

"Yes, Mrs. Stewart. I know I didn't have your permission to leave him in anyone else's charge, but your daughter said it would be all right."

"Of course it's all right," Mrs. Stewart said. "I was just surprised, that's all. Do you intend to be gone very long, Mrs. Duncan?"

"I'll go right back up if you wish."

"No, no, as I said, it's all right."

But it was not all right, Janet felt, as Mrs. Stewart went through the door into the house. For some reason the mother did not want the daughter babysitting with the infant. Or had it simply been surprise that the girl had offered? Janet shrugged, checked her watch, and decided to go ahead and take her walk, but only for thirty minutes, not an hour as the girl had suggested.

MILDRED FOUND herself frowning as she walked swiftly through the narrow side hall. Removing her gloves and hat, she dropped them on the first hall table.

Why was she so distressed to hear that Felicia had gone in to see the baby? Of course it was natural that she would want to see him sometime. As an older sister she would have wanted to see him before this. But to hear that she had sent the nurse away was disturbing to Mildred in a way she did not quite understand. The action carried proprietorship.

She wanted Felicia to love Jeremy, of course. But as a sister, not a mother. The girl must not be touched by scandal. She was a Marchant. She must go back to school, must live in a way that would blot out this shame. And as for baby Jeremy, being brought up as Mildred's son would not deprive him of anything. It was best for everyone, she assured herself, that she had taken this course, made this choice.

*But why did she feel such anxiety knowing that Felicia was alone with her baby?*

She entered the nursery to see them outlined against the light of the open south windows, Felicia's bright hair flowing down her back, her head leaning sideways and resting lightly on the small head of baby Jeremy. They were rocking slowly, and Felicia was murmuring in a sing-song chant, so softly that Mildred could not understand the words. And as she stood there she heard in astonishment an answer, as soft and light as a dove's coo, coming from infant child to mother. It was, Mildred was sure, the first sound he had made. He was talking to Felicia, not crying, but talking in his own way, the best he could, responding as he had not responded to anything or anyone.

Felicia raised her head and looked down at his face, her mouth widening into a smile, into low laughter of delight. Then she raised her head and saw her mother.

"Did you hear him?" she asked. "Did you hear that, Mama? He was answering me."

"It's not possible," Mildred said stiffly. "Babies his age only cry, they don't make other sounds." *But this baby hadn't even cried yet.* Mildred reached for the baby, took him out of Felicia's arms and turned away from the bright face of the girl.

"But he did! I heard him. He was trying to repeat what I was saying. Oh, Mama! What a marvelous thing. Does that mean he's ... normal?"

"Only time will tell that. Why don't you run along, dear, and get some sun? You haven't been out enough this spring. The flowers are blooming and lovely, and the sky is so blue — "

"Why can't I take Jeremy with me?"

"He's much too young to go out, and besides, Felicia, I'd rather you didn't spend more time with him. You need to get your mind on other things." Mildred tried not to see the shadow cross Felicia's face, the bright happiness disappear. It was only a temporary condition, she told herself again. Felicia would be better off in the long run, and so would baby Jeremy, oh, so would he.

She made him comfortable in the cradle, tucking the blanket in around his feet, his tiny body, leaving his hands and arms free. His smoky blue eyes stared up at her disconcertingly, and if she hadn't known better, she would have thought they were filled with anger and hatred. But of course that could not be possible. No baby his age could know these emotions. With God's grace, he would never know them.

Felicia said, "Mama ... how can I get my mind on other things when he needs me and I need him?"

Mildred moved out of sight of the infant boy, put one hand on the hood of the cradle and began rocking it. "*Need him*! That's preposterous, Felicia. You need everything but him. You need freedom to grow up now, to live, to become a woman in mind as well as body. Haven't these past nine months with all the confinement, all the pain and discomfort, taught you anything? You're a child. You made a mistake that does not have to follow you through life. I'm here to absorb that mistake, Felicia, because you are still my child. If you were even two years older, it would be different. But you're not. At the moment he's like a doll to you, but you would grow tired of him quickly, and that would hurt him far more than not seeing and knowing you at all as a mother. Believe me, dear, it's much better for both of you this way. He's your baby brother. Don't ever forget that."

Felicia stood with her head bowed. She picked at her fingernails, as she always did when she was upset about something. Before this, before the past several months, her upsets had been minor ones.

"I won't forget that," she whispered. "But I can't see that it hurts anything if I hold him and talk to him."

Mildred put her arm around Felicia's waist, noting that it still had not gone back to its former slimness, and held her closely as they moved together toward the nursery door. *But I'm right ... I'm right, and someday she will see that.*

"DON'T SEND the nurse away any more dear, please," Mildred said. "She was brought here to take care of Jeremy, and that's her job. When she needs to be relieved I will stay with him. After all, he has to learn that *I'm* his mother, doesn't he?"

Felicia raised her head. "Yes," she said. But the shadow lingered in her eyes, a sadness that she was much too young to know. Mildred felt a moment of sadness at the sight of it, but brought forth her practiced smile. She patted Felicia's back in dismissal.

"Do go on out into the sunshine, dear."

"Yes, Mama."

"You might ride your bicycle to town to see Caroline. You haven't seen her in a long while."

"Since December, Mama," Felicia said patiently, wearily, "when you took me out of school. Don't you remember? I do."

Mildred kept her smile in place with effort. "It would be nice to see an old friend now, wouldn't it, dear? But of course you would be sure to say nothing about — "

"*Mama*. Caroline is probably away for the summer. Her folks are divorced too, and she was already spending her summers with her dad. Anyway, now it would be like trying to make friends with a stranger."

Mildred indulged herself with a sigh. Crowding against the root of her tongue were words that would wound forever. *Stop putting me on the defensive, Felicia. It was you who abandoned yourself to sex with a boy at age thirteen. It was you who brought to me a problem you couldn't even identify. I have done the best I could with it, with you, and now I want you merely to go on being the little girl you are.*

"Go out, Felicia, and at least rest awhile on the terrace. Perhaps tomorrow you'll feel better."

"Yes, ma'am."

As soon as Felicia had left the nursery Mildred started toward her own rooms. She wished now to relax in a hot tub with fragrant bubbles rising around her chin, for hours and hours if necessary, as long as it would take to get the tightness out of her shoulders and the back of her neck. But then she remembered the occupant of the cradle, the object of all the conflict, and she stopped with a small exclamation of impatience. Where was that nurse? And what had she done to deserve this at her age? She went to the nursery telephone and found it dangling on its cord, turning slowly, ever so slowly from one direction to the other, pushed by the breeze from the window. She pulled it up, feeling the tightness increase to dull pain in the back of her neck. She jabbed the button that rang the phone in the kitchen.

"Celta! *Celta.*"

A long moment of silence; Mildred wondered if Celta too had indulged herself with a walk. "Celta!" As though gritting her teeth into the phone and trying to control her voice would bring the elderly servant any faster. She shouldn't be angry with Celta. After all, she was the only one Mildred had dared trust. All others had been discharged months ago, and were just now being replaced. But she wanted only Celta, or the nurse. No one else.

"Celta?"

Finally, "Yes, ma'am?"

Mildred closed her eyes and felt some of the tightness go out of her neck. "Celta, the nurse has taken some time off. Will you please come up to the nursery until she gets back?"

Silence.

"*Celta, are you there*?"

"I'm here," Celta said.

"Did you hear what I said?"

"Yes I heard what you said," Celta replied as she did when she felt she had been pushed too far. At those times they were no longer mistress and servant, but woman and woman, with the elder the superior. "I'll see if I can find the nurse."

Mildred opened her mouth in silence and closed it. Celta made a definite point of slamming her phone down. Mildred replaced hers with care, thoughtfully, envisioning Celta bursting from the house, in her long, stringy stride, to go after the nurse. She had a way of walking, of bending forward and taking very long steps, that indicated her anger. She hated the nursery, and Mildred wasn't sure why. Of course there had been mutters of some kind of old superstition. What had Celta called the child? A changeling. An old-world word for children who weren't normal. No ... not quite that. A superstitious misunderstanding of children who were retarded or otherwise handicapped with deformities or other tragedies. *There are old, old fairies disguised as real bairns. You make him laugh or make him cry and he'll turn into his real form.*

Nonsense, Celta.

*You noticed how he ain't normal. I tell you, best to let the doctor take this one away. There's all kinds of fairies, and some of them are cruel. Evil. They're bewitched. Look at him, he don't never cry.*

Nonsense, *Celta.*

And he was born right after the hour of midnight, and that gives him the power to see the spirits of the dead and of the dark when the fairies come out of the woods and exchange one of their own for a human baby. This here one is of the dark race, the fairy race, I tell you. Changelings are old, old, and they got powers beyond you and me. They can leave their bodies at will and go right through the walls.

No more, Celta. *No more.*

Dark mutters and long strides, body bent forward in the strength of her emotions, her convictions. It was strange, because Celta had been very good with Felicia when she was a baby. Perhaps it simply meant that Celta was getting too old now to be interested in babies. It was time to buy her that plane ticket for Ireland, to let her go home to the land of her dreams.

Mildred looked down into the cradle. The baby was sleeping soundly, as usual, his fists folded against his round cheeks. *Such a good baby.* So very, very good. He never cried, never complained, never demanded. How could Celta be so cruel?

JANET DUNCAN CAME HURRYING BREATHLESSLY into the nursery, her face flushed and moist, the left side of her hair loose from its pins and hanging forward over her cheek.

"I'm so sorry, Mrs. Stewart. I thought ... that is, there's no excuse for my absence. After this I will not leave the baby unless you know about it, and give your permission."

Mildred smiled tightly. "No harm done, Mrs. Duncan." She was already on her way toward her own rooms. "I'm going in to take a long bath, and don't wish to be disturbed."

Janet glanced at the baby, and immediately got busy at the small counter, wiping a formica top that didn't need wiping. From the corner of her eye she saw the door to Mrs. Stewart's private rooms close. At almost the same time she saw the bottle of formula was still in the warmer. The baby hadn't been fed. How many hours had it been? Mother in heaven, where were her senses? She took the bottle from the warmer, shook a drop of milk from it onto her wrist and tasted it. At least it hadn't spoiled. The warmer had merely been doing its job for the hour or so the bottle had been there. Why was it the baby was not screaming for food? She was almost certain he had not been fed since her arrival.

"It's time you're eating, young man," Janet said as she scooped him up. "You can't sleep your life away, you know."

Like most very young babies he balanced nicely on her shoulder, held only by her left arm and hand. With her free hand she gathered up the bottle of formula and a small, soft white towel. It was when she sat down in the rocking chair and slid him further down into the crook of her arm for feeding that she felt the grip on her hair. His tiny fist had become entangled in her loosened hair and was holding fast, pulling her head sideways, bringing tears to her eyes. She dropped the bottle on the floor along with the towel and tried to loosen his fingers. They were boneless little claws, frozen into the grip on her hair. With only one hand available, she could work only awkwardly at best. He lay against her limply and as still as though he were unconscious, but the clutch on her hair seemed to increase rather than lessen. The more she struggled, the tighter he held her. She had to put him back onto her shoulder to take some of the tension out of the pull, to reduce the pain and the involuntary tearing of her eyes. But when she moved him, his body jerked convulsively, once, drawing his arms and legs closer in, wrenching the handful of hair harder, pulling her head as firmly to the side as though she had caught her hair in a vise.

*I can't believe this. I have raised four of my own and taken care of nine grandchildren, to say nothing of all the others I've cared for, and at the worst I've only lost a few strands of hair to a little hand. I was always able to get away without help!*

She felt like crying with frustration, as well as pain, and the tears in her eyes brought up from her throat a sob, low and solitary. She could have cursed, or laughed, for in the moments between effort and frustration, it seemed laughable. She was going to have to go to Mrs. Stewart's bathroom door and cry out for help from the instinctive grip of a baby's hand in her hair! Either that or ...

The scissors were in the drawer of the chest along with the cotton swabs and talcum powder and other items needed in a nursery. With care to cut away only what was necessary, with special care to avoid nicking the soft little knuckles that held her so securely, she freed herself from him. The fist jerked away, the graying strands of hair sticking stiffly from between fingers and thumb.

His eyes were open and looking intently into her face, and it seemed to her that the blueness was malevolent beyond anything in her experience. There was a sound now too, a soft but venomous hissing, and rising from his chest a deep, distant chuckling, evil and antiquated, a sound that could not be human, surely. Then the kind of laughter, and the viperine hissing, were gone again into the recesses from which they had come, so that she wondered at her sanity. Still, she backed away, intimidated, silent. And she knew at that moment she could not stay here, could not keep this job. But of course she would have to give two weeks' notice — that had been understood. For two weeks she would have to feed, bathe, and try to care for this infant.

And the thought of those two weeks formed a knot of sick fear in her throat, her stomach, her heart, for only in physical appearance was this child human.

# CHAPTER 4

Mildred was almost happy. All the waiting seemed now to be over, with the problems resolved. The divorce was final, and not as painful as she had anticipated. Felicia's confinement was over, and she was regaining her health, if ever she had lost it. That was to say, the potential danger to her health was gone. The nurse had arrived, at last, and had taken the worry of the baby off her mind. The weather was grand, when one looked at it through optimistic eyes, and it was a great day to be alive. She stood at the window and breathed deeply of the spring air from the valley and hills, and the flower gardens below her second floor suite. She thought about planning a dinner party. How long had it been since she had entertained guests? Not since she had learned of Felicia's pregnancy, brought to her in a roundabout way from Celta. She would never forget that day as long a she lived, and it came back now to haunt her and detract from her feelings of optimism and of being alive again after these buried months. Celta had come to her as embarrassed as a teenager herself, and they had stood here in this same room, among the fall mums that she was arranging in vases.

. . .

*WHAT IS IT, Celta? You look so undecided and unsure of yourself as though you are coming to me about some great wrong you have done.*

*Yes'm. Well, the truth is, Felicia isn't well these days. She don't really feel like going to school, and I don't think she should. I wonder if maybe you ought to take her to a doctor?*

*Why, what on earth is wrong with her? She hasn't said a word to me.*

*And Celta, looking everywhere but at her, had stammered, well, ma'am, she ain't had a sickness now for a couple of months, and she's sick to her stomach a lot, and — uh — and she was afraid to come to you.*

EVEN NOW SHE felt the shock, the coldness, the stillness that came over her. Those symptoms ... so far away in her past, but so unforgettable. God in Heaven. Felicia? She wouldn't be fourteen until the third of November, and this was still October. She was thirteen, for God's sake, and had never dated a boy in her life. Had she?

Obviously she had, but without Mildred's knowledge or consent. It was this kind of thing that made mothers so afraid of every boy who looked at her daughters. Mildred wondered who the father was. Which of the skinny little bike-riding brats had done this to her daughter? And why, for the love of God, had Felicia let him. She was a Marchant; she should have had more pride. Or were girls simply different these days?

Perhaps she should have talked of sex with Felicia. Warned her? But they were saying these days, don't turn your daughter against sex, don't make her feel it's wrong. So therefore Mildred had said nothing.

Which one was it? The boy with the red hair and freckles — Gary Appleby, was that his name? Or the little dark-haired boy who lived out of town? Not one of them was taller than Felicia herself; all of them were children still.

She hadn't asked then who the father was. *Father?* It was ludicrous. Those little twerps fathers!

And she would never ask now.

She wanted only to forget. She wanted her little girl to behave. She wanted to live again, to travel to New York City, or to Paris, or London, to have dinner parties again, to follow the sun, and sometimes the snow. She longed to ski, to swim, to forget.

She went to her desk and began to draw up a list. Perhaps, she decided, she would invite her brother and his current lady friend down from New York for a weekend. She would call him later, and explain to him that she hadn't felt like talking with anyone for months, even her only brother, Martin, because of the final breakup of her marriage, and her pregnancy. But now the divorce was final, and the baby was born, and she felt alive again.

Not even Martin would be told the truth about Jeremy. It was none of his business. It was nobody's business.

She would invite her attorney, James Wellington and his wife, Martha, even though Martha was a bit of a problem to serve since she was a recovered alcoholic and a diabetic too, so that she not only dared not touch a cocktail or dinner wine, but adhered to a strict diet. Poor Martha.

She would ask Clarence and Jack and Polly. They had stopped calling her, and no wonder. She might find now that she had no friends left, after so many months of avoiding them. Fortunately very few of her friends lived in Jonesboro, so no one ever dropped in unexpectedly.

Her sitting room, cream walls and rose and cream floral carpets, had turned golden from the last rays of the setting sun. She pulled the draperies and turned on a table lamp at the end of the sofa. She decided to dress for dinner, even though her only companion would be Felicia, and she would probably be in her everlasting denim jeans.

She entered her large dressing room and spent an hour choosing a dinner gown. She took dozens off the racks, and replaced them, and finally grew tired of the game and chose a simple ecru satin and lace gown with jeweled buttons from bust to knees, and with a sexy slit below. Her enthusiasm was beginning to wane. What she really needed was to go shopping, spend two or three weeks replacing last year's clothes. Instead of asking everyone to come here, perhaps she should wrangle an invitation out of Martin and go to New York.

Or, better still, why didn't she just go to Paris for a few days, now that Janet Duncan had arrived and seemed so capable?

She thought of Paris as she dressed, as she applied makeup automatically. She needed a new haircut. She needed many things.

Ready for dinner, thinking of Paris, she went out into the hallway. Janet, in an old blue chenille robe, was waiting for her.

"Mrs. Stewart," Janet Duncan said with an abrupt movement toward her that caused Mildred to stop warily. "I want to give my two weeks' notice. I just simply can't accept this job after all."

"But you only arrived today," Mildred said, composure slipping beneath surprise. "I thought — I understood that you wanted the position."

"I did. But I find now I can't stay. I'm sorry."

"Perhaps after you rest a few days, you'll feel better about it. Whatever we can do, Mrs. Duncan, to make the work easier, we'll be glad to do. Just ask Celta when you need help."

"No," Janet Duncan said. She looked at the dinner gown Mildred was wearing and felt ugly in comparison. "It's not that I feel the work is strenuous, Mrs. Stewart. I'm very sorry, but I must give my two weeks' notice today. I would leave tomorrow if you had someone else available to take over the — uh — the nursing. As you know, I'm a practical nurse, not an RN, and I don't feel I'm qualified for the job."

Mildred saw, with a sense of drowning, all her plans going awry.

"But why, for goodness' sake? What could possibly make you feel inadequate? It isn't necessary that you be a registered nurse. I was aware that you weren't when I hired you."

"Mrs. Stewart," Janet said, "your little son has a medical problem that I don't feel I can handle."

*Oh God, not now,* thought Mildred. *Don't tell me something I already know, and which is none of your goddamned business.*

"A medical problem? Because he coughed up on you? Babies do those things occasionally. I assure you, Mrs. Duncan, that it was the first time it has happened, and it may never happen again."

"I wasn't thinking of that. There's another problem. He goes into something similar to — to — well, perhaps a mild seizure. Perhaps it's a forerunner of epilepsy. I don't know. That's the trouble, you see, it's beyond my experience."

"Oh. Is it a limpness, a total relaxation of body, you're concerned about?"

"Why, yes. I guess that's a fair description."

Mildred smiled tightly. "I think he's simply a lazy baby, Janet. He was born in exactly that condition, and scarcely moved for hours. It amounts to nothing at all but a very sound sleep. Don't let it worry you." She put out a neatly manicured hand and brushed Janet's sleeve reassuringly. "Goodnight, Janet. Tomorrow you'll be more rested."

She started on, but Janet followed her a few steps.

"Mrs. Stewart, please go ahead and replace me as soon as you can. I'll be leaving in two weeks."

Mildred Stewart paused, but did not look around. After a moment she said, "All right, Mrs. Duncan. Feel free to leave whenever you choose. I'm sure I'll have no trouble replacing you."

Janet felt as though a great load had been taken off her shoulders. She went back into the nursery and closed the door. The baby in the cradle was silent, and she went only close enough to see that he was still covered. She turned out the lights, entered her bedroom and prepared for a long, uneasy night.

*Why didn't I tell Mrs. Stewart the real reason I want to leave? I'm afraid of your son ... There's something about him that terrifies me ... that makes me doubt my own sanity ... If I hadn't given my word, I would leave here tonight, even if I had to walk all the way back to town.*

Janet sat on the bed and wished she dared take a sleeping pill. But of course she had to be awake for the two o'clock feeding.

AFTER FELICIA FINISHED dinner she asked to be excused to go into the family room to watch television. Mildred, left alone at the table in the breakfast room, invited Celta to have a glass of wine with her.

Celta filled two glasses and sat down across from Mildred, watching her light another cigarette from the remains of the first.

Mildred said, "I have problems, Celta."

"Ummhummm."

"Janet Duncan is leaving. I can't believe that she would give notice on her first day, but she did."

Celta watched Mildred smoke, the gray curling diaphanous curtain hanging between them. She had been smoking more and more this past year and it worried Celta, but she did not comment on it. This new worry was too unexpected.

"Leaving? But she just got here."

"I know. But I couldn't talk her out of it. She said she felt inadequate for the job. She said he has medical problems she can't handle."

"And what's that?"

"Seizures, she calls them. She thinks he has a form of epilepsy, I believe."

"Hummum."

"Is that all you have to say?"

"What did you tell her?"

"That he simply sleeps very soundly. You don't think he has that kind of problem, do you, Celta?"

"No," Celta said emphatically. "I've seen epilepsy, in Dublin, before I came here. No, it's not that."

"Well. I think she's probably sorry she left home, and is looking for any excuse she can find. Whatever her reasons, it puts me in a very awkward position. I was going to buy you a plane fare back home, Celta, and arrange a retirement fund for you so you could go back to Ireland, but now I need you, and just simply can't do without you at this time. Of course, if you want very much to go ..."

"It's close to forty years since I saw relatives or friends in Ireland. We wouldn't know one another anymore. This is my home now; as long as you need me, I'll stay."

Mildred clasped Celta's hand for a moment. "Oh thank you, dear. I hate imposing on you, but I do need you. If this nurse leaves before I can get another, I must ask you to fill her place."

Celta shook her head. "I'll do all his laundry, and everybody else's. I'll clean the floors, dust the furniture, and even do all the cooking, just like I've been doing the last few months. But I won't be a nursemaid any more. You'll just have to find somebody else."

Mildred gave Celta a hard stare. "I don't understand this! Why are you so reluctant to take care of that tiny baby?"

Celta shrugged a bony shoulder. "I told you, and you didn't believe me. Now I say, you get that nurse to tell you the real reason she's leaving, and I'll bet you it ain't got nothing to do with any medical problems. That bairn gives a body the creeps, that's what it is."

"Nonsense, Celta! The poor little mite is probably mentally retarded, that's all."

"That's the first time I've heard you say that."

"It's something I have no wish to talk about. And it's nobody's business. When a nurse is paid to clean, feed, and care for a baby in a general way, that's all she needs to be concerned about. Of course I won't ask you to take over the care of him as you did Felicia, but there may be days between nurses, if this is an example, when I'll need you in the nursery."

Celta gave another dogged, negative shake of her head. "No, not me. One of the downstairs maids can go up, and I'll do her job down here as well as my own. I'm not nursing any more little wee bairns, and especially not that one."

Mildred said, "Try to eliminate those horrible old fairy tales from your mind for a while, Celta, and give me a logical reason that I can accept. Why is he so difficult to be around?"

"A logical reason!" Celta retorted. "How can give you a logical reason when there ain't none?

"That's what I thought," Mildred said coolly as she rose from the table. "There *is* no reason! I'm going upstairs. Goodnight."

Celta watched Mildred leave the room and knew she would never understand. Only one person understood: Janet Duncan. But of course Celta would never discuss it with her. Not with hired help.

She got up to join Felicia in the family room.

JANET DUNCAN SLEPT RESTLESSLY. There was no sound from the nursery. She woke frequently, listening, wishing to hear a good healthy cry, demand for attention. She would rather spend the night walking the floor with a fussing infant than to be smothered by the unnatural quiet.

At two o'clock she got wearily out of bed and went into the nursery. She turned on a lamp on the counter beside the refrigerator and got a bottle of milk. The bottle was cold, chilling her hand, but instead of slipping it into the warmer she carried it with her across the room to the cradle. He didn't look as though he had changed positions, and he was sleeping quietly and peacefully. He'd had his last bottle at six o'clock, held up against his face by a small quilted bottle holder she'd found tucked away in a drawer. It was unusual that one his age did not wake up at night, hungry. But he was sleeping, and she felt relieved. After a few minutes of watching him, of seeing no signs of wakefulness, she put the bottle back into the refrigerator and turned out the lights.

Since it looked as though he was going to sleep the night through, she felt safe now in taking a sleeping pill. There seemed no other way to get a restful sleep.

She was going quietly from the nursery, eager now for the medication she kept only for emergencies, when a movement at the cradle drew her attention, and a sound, as of a long sigh, or, more precisely, a soft wind being drawn through a narrow tunnel. She turned and looked back into the darkened nursery. The only light came from her bathroom and, reduced by distance, left a gloom, a murkiness, that increased in the area of the cradle, obscuring its outlines.

At first she saw nothing. The area surrounding the cradle seemed more shadowed, darker than it had before. He must have awakened, she decided, disturbed perhaps by the soft closing of the refrigerator door, and the light she had turned on and then off. He had moved, she was sure. He had sighed ... or was it the wind beyond the window. Or the swaying of a tree limb brushing against the house?

She wanted to go on to her bathroom and find comfort in the bright fluorescent light that blazed above the mirror. She wanted to take her sleeping pill, and not wake up again until the sun was high in the sky.

But conscience pulled her back. If the baby had awakened, she would have to give him his bottle. He was too tiny, too young to go all night without nourishment.

The cradle seemed to have changed shape, the hood with the blue netting bulging higher than she had noticed before. The realization came slowly to her, as something so gradual it was almost unnoticeable. She stopped, her flesh chilling in the warm air of the closed room. The blue netting of the hood had risen, was now rising even as she watched, as her eyes adjusted to the shadows in this silent room. As though lifted by the soft almost soundless wind, the netting was drifting upward away from the cradle, separating from the cradle to float in the air ...

She did not move. She watched, stared and saw it was not the netting, but an object that had broken free from somewhere below the hood. A faint, blue, misty form that was slowly takin shape and becoming ... dear God ... the baby himself... or a kind of reflection of him … almost invisible ... moving now. Turning.

*Turning.*

*Seeing her.*

*Coming toward her.*

*Floating on his stomach above the hood of the cradle, yet closer, closer, his head tilted upright like the head of a snake, and his eyes beginning to glow in the dark, the evil thrusting at her, drawing toward her, the nearly invisible blue body trailing behind the head with a reptilian curl ...*

She sucked her breath in harshly and tried to scream, to cry out for help, but as in a nightmare all she could do was choke on her own thickened tongue and swollen throat. She was not aware that her feet moved, that she was able to move at all, and her progress was heavy and clumsy as she turned her back upon the apparition that was drifting toward her. The bright light in the half-opened door of the bathroom seemed to be her savior, and her arms went out toward it as her body awkwardly stumbled forward. As though a miracle had happened she reached that rectangle of light and fell forward onto her knees. She twisted about onto her buttocks, on the cool, polished tile of the bathroom floor, and slammed the door shut. Sobbing, gasping for air, she leaned against the door, holding it, and finally reaching up with a weak and trembling hand to snap the lock shut. And hoped, prayed, it would help.

The only sound was her own tortured gasps.

Gradually she calmed. The nausea caused by the nightmare panic eased away. She sat with her ear against the door, and heard nothing. She began murmuring to herself.

"I've got to get out of here. Now. Tonight. I can throw my things together and be on my way in two minutes. I'll walk. I'd rather be out on the dark road than in this house with that thing. Whatever it is. And I'll make the doctor understand what I've seen if I have to drag him down here and let him see it for himself. Something has got to be done. It has to be stopped before it goes any farther. Whatever it is ... whatever ..."

Her own voice reassured her, and she rose from the cool floor of the bathroom and slowly opened the door, putting her head out with utmost caution, looking around from one shadowed corner of the bedroom to the other.

It was gone.

The room looked as innocuous as her bedroom at home, but she moved into it with a sense of urgency she had never experienced before. Looking over one shoulder, and then the other, she hastily dressed and threw the rest of her clothes into her largest bag, stuffing them down in such a messy pile that it seemed for a moment she would not be able to close it. With nervous hands she threw the lid back and poked articles deeper into the corners until she managed to fasten it. And then a glance over her shoulder toward the darkened corner that joined the nursery near the bathroom froze her.

Slowly, as though peeling itself away from its own body, surrounded by the faint blue light that was scarcely more than a mist in the darkness, the head of the creature was coming through the wall. Its eyes were upon her, burning with outrage and malevolence, its tongue darting, hissing — at her, and she had one swift thought before all rationality left her: *he heard me ... he heard what I said ...* She stood immobilized until it had come almost entirely through the wall, the diaphanous blue tail trailing, curling virulently behind the head. Small appendages were appearing at the upper end of the body, and were becoming arms, and hands, and they were reaching for her, pointed fingers curled into claws.

She ran.

She struck the banisters in the hallway, and they saved her from falling to the floor fourteen feet below. On the stairway she stumbled and fell onto her knees and rolled several steps before she regained her balance. She looked back: it was coming behind her, slithering low, keeping to the darkness against the steps, its tail undulating, as though serpent-like, it had become its means of locomotion.

She reached the heavy front door, wrenched it open, slammed it shut behind her, as though it might help, might in some way contain him. And then she ran desperately through pale streaks of moonlight that filtered through the trees onto the driveway. It wasn't until she reached the road to town that she noticed she carried the heavy bag, and she knew she should drop it, but her hand was frozen on the handle. She ran on with it bumping against her leg.

The moonlight was left behind at the first curve in the road as the forest leaned, touching above, tall treetops intertwining. She ran through darkness, her footsteps slapping against the macadam and exploding in her ears, her breath burning and bursting from her lungs. She didn't look back. She wouldn't pause to look back until she had reached town, two miles away. Less now, less, perhaps a mile away, now.

She didn't have to look back to know that it had caught up with her. She saw the blue glow first, as though someone had shone a pale blue light at the back of her head.

And then it was winding around her neck, choking her, cutting off all oxygen.

She stumbled and fell to her knees, and raised both hands to claw at it. The blue light now blinded her bulging eyes. His face, so close against hers, forced her back and down. Her hands clawed, feebly, but there was nothing of substance to grasp. Her writhing body struck her spilled suitcase, and scattered white uniforms across the black, hard road, ghostly glimmers in the dark night.

MILDRED WOKE EARLY, lost for a moment in a fading nightmare, an unpleasant dream she couldn't recall. Then she came sharply awake and knew it wasn't a dream, but reality. The nurse, Janet Duncan, had given two weeks' notice, and today she had to start all over again.

She went into the bathroom and looked at herself in the mirror, critically. A few more years, and she would have to have a facelift, and she was too damned young to be thinking about that!

With Janet's record, her experience, she would be hard to replace. Maybe, if she went to her, offered more money, she would stay.

Mildred drew a long-sleeved, heavy robe closely about her even though the day promised to be very warm, and went down the narrow passageway that connected her suite to the nursery.

She passed by the cradle without looking into it, and went to the open doorway of the bedroom. She stopped. The bed was still turned down, unmade, and no one was in it. There was something about the room, the untidiness, the silence, that alarmed her. She moved slowly into the center of the room, looked from the four-poster bed to the dressing table, with its three-way mirrors, to the bathroom. The door there stood open, the light on. It took only a glance to see that it was empty, as empty as the closet, as the drawers in the chest that matched the dressing table. The suitcases were gone. No, a small one had been left. And the overnight case. And a few odds and ends.

But Janet Duncan was gone.

"*Goddamn!*"

Mildred cursed under her breath. She turned a circle in the room, but Janet Duncan did not materialize.

"*Oh, damn!*"

She had gone without saying goodbye, go to hell, or anything. What had been her hurry? When had she left? It must have been before daylight, Mildred concluded, because the bathroom light had not been turned out.

That meant the baby hadn't been taken care of at all.

Mildred went into the nursery and with quick, nervous, angry movements, took up the wet, cold infant from the cradle. First, a bottle of formula into the warmer, and while he sucked one fist alternately after the other, a quick bath followed by warm clothes. Then, when he was clean and dry and the bottle of milk was warm, she disregarded her own orders and returned him to the cradle, propping the bottle against his face. When she left him the baby was sucking eagerly and hungrily. She didn't notice that his eyes followed her as far as he could see her.

Back in her sitting room, she dialed her attorney's home number. He wouldn't have gone to his office yet. In fact, he might not even be out of bed yet. Too bad. She was not interested in other people's problems at the moment.

He drowsily answered the phone. She said, "That nurse you got for me was a fiasco, James. She's gone, sometime during the night. If this is an example of what I'm going to have to put up with, I think I'll find another lawyer."

"Left?" he said, awakening. "But that's not possible. She was supposed to be most reliable."

"Well, she wasn't. Get me someone as fast as you can. If we have to raise the salary, then do it. I need a babysitter if I can't get a nurse. I can just see the months going by, and no one here to help me with the baby. I have other things to do, James. Find someone to take care of him!" She hung up angrily, then rang the kitchen. No one answered. After waiting impatiently, she slammed the phone down and went out into the hall to call for Celta. But before she could open her mouth, Celta's own voice came screeching up from the lower hall.

"Mildred! Mildred, Clint's down here! Something dreadful has happened to Janet Duncan! On his way out from town he found her, right in the middle of the road — " Celta was coming up the stairs in a long, stooped lope, talking, looking up at Mildred, who stood by the banisters above, "with her suitcase open and her clothes scattered all around her, and she had been murdered! What she was doing out on the road ... I reckon she was walking to town ... you'd better come on down. Clint's calling the police, and they'll want to ask you what she was doing out on the road, who she was — " Celta, having reached the top of the stairs, turned abruptly and ran down again, leaving Mildred staring at the top of her head.

This news, so chillingly unexpected, drove from Mildred's thoughts all else. She forgot that she needed Celta to stay with the baby again. She forgot the baby entirely. Slowly, she went downstairs to wait for the police. But what could she tell them? Janet Duncan had come to work for her, but had decided suddenly that she wanted to go home. If she had waited until Clint arrived he would have driven her to the airport. But as it was ...

There had never been a murder in Jonesboro district in all her memory, before this.

. . .

LIKE A DISTURBED BEEHIVE the small town of Jonesboro buzzed with the news. The people gathered on the cool, shaded town square around the courthouse, where benches had been placed generations ago for the comfort of the people, and talked about it, passing information along.

*SAID SHE WAS STRANGLED, but her eyes were gouged out too, and there were a lot of scratches on her face. But the odd thing about that was, and I've got it directly from the county coroner, the scrapings under her fingernails were from her own flesh!*

*She's a northerner, they said. Just come down here to work for the Marchants. Clay Turner says he remembers right well driving her out to Tanglewood just a couple of days ago, but said she was mighty close-mouthed and didn't tell him nothing except she was going to nurse somebody at the Marchants, at Tanglewood.*

*Nurse somebody! Is somebody sick out there?*

*Well, you know the young Marchant girl ain't been in school this year at all.*

*Felicia Stewart? Her name ain't Marchant.*

*You know who I mean. And Mildred Marchant herself ain't been seen around here for months.*

*Well, don't you know she's been away? And the girl was sent to some fancy school in Europe, or somewhere, they said. Clay probably got his wires crossed, and that woman was just going out there to work in the kitchen or something.*

*There were white nurse uniforms scattered on the road. Why would kitchen help wear nurse uniforms?*

THE SHERIFF DIDN'T KNOW any more than the townspeople. There was no clue at all as to the killer. He didn't know which way to turn, and finally filed it away. The body was sent home, and the blood washed off the road. The people at Tanglewood, the old woman, Celta, the chauffeur, Clint, and Mildred Marchant herself could tell him nothing. Janet Duncan had left, and had been murdered by someone who found her walking the dark road to town.

Case closed.

You never knew about these out-of-town people, these northerners. She might have had connections with the Mafia, or someone who was out to kill her.

# CHAPTER 5

He was calling her in his voiceless way. The touch of the tiny, cold hands on her face, waking her, no longer frightened her quite so much as it had. Mostly, now, it was not knowing when the touch would come, or where, or why. Sometimes she felt the small hands on her arm, touching firmly and fading away, like a snowflake melting. Sometimes on her throat, clutching softly. There was only one thing, one condition, she could be sure of: the darkness. At first there had been faltering half touches during the day, as though he weren't sure of himself yet, as though he were searching out a kind of pathway toward her, but he moved in darkness as naturally as a creature going home. In the shadowy half-dark of twilight or dawn, in the deep black of a cloud-covered night, or when the moon spilled its alien pale white light into her room to create paths between the threatening dark shadows cast by chair, by bed, by the window itself, then the touches came; and at other time she waited, her breath jerking softly in a kind of anticipatory dread, her mind and heart conflicting between tender love and numbing fear.

The night was very dark this time, and still, as though waiting. The touch came in her deepest sleep, jerking her out of it as though she had been shot. Yet the hand lay soft on her neck. Her face was turned toward the rectangle of western windows, and for a nerveless moment after the touch left her, she stared at its paler black. A thin thread of lightning, too far away for its repercussions to be heard, moved crossways in the sky. Silence was very deep, inside the house and out. Even the owls had taken shelter from the threat of the approaching storm.

Felicia turned onto her side and switched on her bedside lamp. Her door was firmly closed, and even locked. She had taken to locking it recently; she wasn't quite sure why. Yet always, it seemed, she expected to find it standing open. It was the first thing she looked at when she turned the light on at night, after the strange little hands had touched her.

After he had called her to him.

She left her room without slippers or robe, and without light. The hallways were caverns of blackness through which she felt her way, finding familiar corners where she had found them before, and edges of rugs, and smooth sides of furniture, all landmarks in her dark nightly trek to the nursery. Everyone was sleeping. Even the new nurse was sleeping. Felicia entered her room and paused by her bed to make sure she was soundly asleep, and saw the unfamiliar face in the low light cast by a table lamp. In the three months since Jeremy's birth so many nurses had occupied this small bedroom that Felicia no longer bothered to try to remember the names. She called them Nurse, and, she noticed, so did her mother. Felicia smiled to herself. Funny, how the nurses came and went.

Another nightlight was soft in the nursery, with just enough illumination to show the nurse her way about if she had to get up with the baby during the night. But she never did, for it was Felicia whom baby Jeremy called.

The cradle was turned away from the light so that the hood cast a shadow upon the baby's face. Felicia bent over the cradle and looked in, and met the direct stare of the dark blue eyes, shadowed by the hood of his cradle and his long, feathery lashes. She smiled, and slipped her hands under his plump little body. "My baby," she whispered, for always now she whispered to him. Their meetings were secret, more and more as days and nights went by. "Felicia's baby boy, darling baby. Felicia's here. Are you hungry?" He hadn't heard baby talk from Felicia, only from various nurses. Hearing them talk to him, saying things like, "Oh, is him an itsy bitsy boy today? Does him want his bobby boo from the moo cow now?" made her lips curl involuntarily with disgust. She had been struck with the silliness of it, and knew in the depths of her heart that Jeremy hated it. But then, he hated his nurses too, didn't he?

She gathered him warm into her arms, feeling him meld with the curve of her breast and stomach, his head lying under her chin against her throat, his tummy curving over her breast, his plump knees pushing in to her diaphragm. She brought a thin, summer blanket up from a folded stack on the chest and covered them both from chin down. And she whispered to him.

"We'll look out the window at the pretty lightning while your milk warms, and then we'll sit and rock and let the storm come, and you won't ever be afraid, because you're in Felicia's arms, now."

She followed her own predictions, slowly, putting the bottle of milk into the warmer and going to stand in front of the window. The lightning was closer now, and the soft, long murmurs of thunder were coming through the windows, from the heavy layers of clouds that were underlined by the flashes of light. It was like the guts of a mattress hanging above them, with wads of cotton slipping down, ugly grays, soft grays, like the one she had seen in the attic once a long time ago. She was not afraid of the storm. She had never been afraid of storms. And neither was Jeremy, she knew.

She brought his milk from the warmer and sat down in the rocking chair by the window. She smiled when she saw the greed with which the little pink mouth opened and reached for the nipple. With a sigh of contentment she settled back and watched him as he sucked, and listened both to the softly rolling thunder and the sounds he made.

Always before he took the bottle his mouth turned toward her breast, telling her his preference, and she wished from the depths of her soul that it could have been that way. Still, she got to hold him, and feed him, at night. They never allowed her to feed him in the daytime. Only occasionally could she persuade the current nurse to let her do the feeding. Then, when Mother found out, the nurse would start refusing. However, none of the nurses stayed long enough for it to become a problem.

It had been a good summer. One of the best in her memory. Baby Jeremy had filled in all the empty spots, so that she didn't even miss her father as much as she thought she would. Of course, even in summers gone by, he hadn't been around that much. His business had taken him to foreign countries and other states so that at times he seemed more a guest than a family member. This year she had been too busy with Jeremy, too filled with his existence, to spend much time thinking about anyone else. She hadn't even wanted to go swimming in the river. She much preferred taking Jeremy for a walk through the gardens, and into the woods. He loved the forest, that spreading, deep, shadowed, cool place where the tree trunks rose around you like pillars to the sky, where the sky itself was only an occasional blue star far above and beyond the green roof of the forest. In there they had found little springs of water coming under gray, solid bluffs, edged by little carpets of soft moss. Jeremy liked the moss. His tiny fingers clutched the moss so hard she could hardly remove them, and when she brought him back to the house her mother had seen, and knew they had been walking in the woods, and had become angrier than Felicia had ever seen her. She'd snatched the baby away, and he had thrown up all over her. Remembering now, Felicia smiled. And baby Jeremy drew away from his nipple and gave her an answering milky, toothless smile from a wide-open mouth. A delighted, hilarious smile that brought soft giggles to Felicia's throat.

Felicia hugged him to her, and kissed the top of his head, that silky, soft hair that was the color of her own. The lightning came closer as they rocked, the thunder beginning now to jar the window with sound and bringing large raindrops that struck with force and splattered to run down blurring the flashing landscape beyond.

MILDRED WOKE WITH A JOLT. Even though her draperies were drawn, the flashes of lightning penetrated the room and gave her the chills that lightning and thunder always did. She curled drawing her knees to her chest, turning her back to the windows. Her lightweight blanket was not enough to keep the chills away, to make her feel al all secure. She thought of getting up to find another one, and dreaded getting out of bed. She curled tighter.

The baby ...

Would that nurse, that half-wit who had let Felicia take the baby into the forest again, get up and take care of him? If she were at all afraid of storms she probably would not. And Jeremy would probably be terrified. Poor baby. He would never cry out. He never cried. Only occasionally did he even whimper. He was such a good baby.

*Such a good baby.*

With a groan Mildred got out of bed, turned on the light, and slipped into a warm robe. Then she went into the hallway toward the nursery.

They were so quiet that at first she didn't see them, cuddled together in the large rocker by the window. At first she saw only the windows that were being bombarded by rain and lightning, and with a low curse on her lips for the nurse, she rushed to draw the blinds. Then she forgot the windows.

"Felicia! What on earth are you doing here at this time of night?"

The girl looked up at her calmly, unsmiling. "I'm giving him his bottle," she said.

Mildred stood helplessly looking down. The baby was held with maternal possessiveness against the young breast, and the bottle was almost empty. That meant Felicia had been feeding him for some time now.

"Then — why — " Mildred was stammering, feeling confused and angry and helpless. "Why hadn't you closed the blinds?"

"I'm not afraid of the storm. It's really very beautiful, Mama, look. See how the clouds tumble in the light? And how the trees are so wet and green, and bright one moment and gone in darkness the next? A storm is beautiful."

"Well I don't think so!" Mildred jerked the blinds down ferociously, one after the other. Long chills ran down her body, like the rain down the windows. "I don't understand why you're here at all, feeding him," she said. "The nurses all say that he never takes a bottle at night — "

Suddenly she knew, and was amazed at her slowness. All these nights it had been Felicia who gave the baby his feeding, and the stupid, logy-headed nurses hadn't even known.

"You've been feeding him!" she accused, and made it sound like a crime. She felt fear along with her anger, and could not understand it. What difference did it make? And yet it did.

Felicia put the question into words. Softly. "Mama, what difference does it make? Why can't I give him his two o'clock feeding?"

Mildred stood before them trembling with emotions she couldn't untangle. She folded her arms under her breasts and clutched each forearm in a cold hand, yet the chills kept coming. It was a coldness brought by strong emotions, and by fear, she knew. Fear of the storm? No, it was more than that. It wasn't that she was afraid the baby would love Felicia more, no it wasn't that. It was Felicia herself that was the center of her concern, her fear ... But why?

She deliberately softened and calmed her voice. "Then you've been feeding the baby all along?"

"Yes, for a couple of months."

Mildred stared down at them, at the contented baby whose eyes were closing now, whose mouth was relaxing around the nipple of the bottle, at the pale oval face of the girl raised toward her. They were both so beautiful, so young, so innocent that it made her heart ache. One a miniature of the other, except for the sex.

"Every night," Mildred said in amazement, "you've been getting up and coming all the way to the nursery? How did you know when to come?"

"He called me."

"Called you! Felicia, that is not possible."

"But he does, Mama! Only not with his voice, with his hands. He comes to me, and touches me, and I know he wants me. So I come to him, and he's always waiting, and awake."

"Felicia," Mildred drew a long sigh. "My dear, you've been dreaming, you realize that, don't you?"

"That's what I thought at first. When it first started happening. I thought it had to have been a dream, even though it didn't seem like it. But they aren't dreams, Mama. Honest."

Mildred drew up a chair and sat down near Felicia. She drew her robe even more tightly around her freezing body, and tried to rub the goosebumps from her arms. They were going to have a serious talk, and Mildred didn't even know where to start. Felicia obviously was alone too much ... or had the birth of the child done something to her mind?

"Are you cold, Mama?"

"It's the storm. They always give me chills. I wonder how on earth that nurse can sleep through all this? There's not only the storm, but our voices!"

Felicia looked down at her baby and smiled faintly. "She won't last long. She'll be just like all the others."

"It doesn't really matter. Since I raised the salary, new nurses are very easy to come by. Especially since I also lowered the qualifications. I've become adjusted; I'm going to need to keep an eye on whoever is nursing him." The words were automatic, needing no prior thought. They had stood up under the test of three months. Her thoughts were a different matter, a confused jumble aroused by Felicia's calm statement about Jeremy. "Felicia, dear, about those dreams ..."

"Not dreams, Mama. Somehow, he touches me, and I feel it. And it wakes me —"

"Wakes you! See, you're always asleep when this happens, so it must be a combination of dreams and imagination. Whatever it is, leave the night feedings to a nurse. That's what they're here for."

"But why?" Anguish was in her voice. "Why can't I feed him and hold him, especially at night, Mama? What difference does it make?"

Instead of answering her, Mildred looked at the sleeping baby. "Why don't you put him back into his cradle now and go on back to bed? I'll just sit here for a while. I can't sleep anyway when it's storming like this."

Without another word Felicia lay the baby in his cradle, tucked the blankets lovingly around him, and left the room.

Mildred sat listening to the storm pound the house like some great and vicious monster trying to break in. How was it that storms could intimidate her so terribly, and not affect her daughter at all? Her own flesh and blood. Her second self. Felicia was her only child, because she had wanted it that way. She had been ever careful from that one birth on to make sure it didn't happen again. It wasn't that she didn't like children, she told herself. It was just that babies grew up to become teenagers and young people who needed yet rejected guidance, and brought to her a feeling of helplessness she hated. She had been in control of her own life much too long to accept defeat gracefully. Yet now all her plans seemed to be going awry. Felicia was disobeying her. Subtly, but surely.

The storm was moving on at last, crashing not so much against the walls as overhead and farther away. The baby was sleeping without sound.

The answer came to her as though someone had knocked on a door in her memory: Miss Westchester's school for girls. A memory from her childhood focused suddenly and clearly. A tall red brick building, as austere as a jail, separated from a quiet street only by a row of old trees, with six steps leading up to the heavy, tall, front door. And inside, polished wood floors, no carpets, polished stair banisters, plain white walls, and a strong, severe face behind the neat desk in the office. Miss Westchester herself was no longer there, but her successors were just as strict, just as demanding as Miss Westchester could ever have been. Westchester girls did not get into trouble. Mildred had spent two years there, coming out at age fifteen when her mother died. Two or three years at Miss Westchester's — that was the answer for Felicia!

Mildred drew a long sigh of relief and left the window to return to her own room. She felt as though a great burden had been lifted from her shoulders. The chills were also gone. She was comfortable again, at ease.

At the doorway she remembered the baby, and turned back to check on him. As she bent over the cradle she saw that his eyes were open and watching her, his small face round and fair against the blue blankets beneath and above him, his eyes seeming unusually dark in the shadows cast by the hood. Her hands began tucking blankets, automatically, closer about his body, under his arms, around his feet.

"Go back to sleep now, that's a good little boy, Ummhuh."

She bent down to kiss his forehead, relieved of so many burdens that her heart felt a touch of tenderness. The storm had moved on, the thunder now deep rumbles instead of crashes, and tomorrow she would arrange to send Felicia to Miss Westchester's and —

It came suddenly and unexpectedly, full in her face, spraying with such force that it stung and pierced her skin, covering her eyes and hair and running down between her breasts to wet her nightgown, curds and whey of milk so rotten they could have been centuries old. She jerked back, blinded. When she straightened the horror ran into her mouth, bitter and revolting, and for a moment she felt as though her own vomit would be added to it. She turned groping for the bathroom, for water and washcloth, and managed to clear her eyes and mouth. Above the wash basin she saw herself in the mirror of the medicine cabinet, and was shocked. Her hair was hanging in wet strings around her face, with bits of white clinging like maggots. Her face was slimy horrible. Anger flared. With a clean washcloth she mopped furiously, with little result. This was the second time he had spit up on her ... *spit up*? What an ineffectual expression for such a revolting mess!

She threw the washcloth down and went after the nurse. As she passed the cradle there was soft, deep, guttural laughter, as evil as a forbidden act, as vile as his vomit. She stopped, astonished and the chills returned to pull at her skin. She could not look into the cradle. Laughter? No, of course not, reason told her. It was the thunder, rolling and drifting farther and farther away, it was part of the storm, not of baby Jeremy. It was scarcely his fault if his milk sometimes disagreed with him. He was a good baby. A Marchant baby.

She went on, as chilled as though the storm had reversed itself with a vengeance and was headed directly for her. The nurse lay with her mouth opened toward the ceiling, emitting almost masculine snores. Perhaps, Mildred muttered to herself, that was what she had heard! She clutched the plump shoulder without preliminary warning.

"Miss — uh — *Nurse*! Will you wake up, please!"

The young woman in the bed gurgled to silence and her eyes looked for a moment as though they would pop out of her head. She jerked away, clambering across the bed toward the wall like a crawfish backing under a rock.

Mildred exclaimed in exasperation, "Forever more, Nurse! It's only me. Have you not been aware at all that we've been having a dreadful storm? A baby needs attention at a time like this!"

The nurse was hunched on the far side of the bed, looking attentively at Mildred's milk-curdled hair, her blotched face and neck. The smell could not be ignored.

"What on earth happened?" she asked, openly puzzled, yet with a touch of amusement showing at the corners of her mouth. "Don't tell me the baby did that!"

"And where else do you think I would get into this kind of mess? Naturally, he needs cleaning up now. I would appreciate some help from you," Mildred said furiously. She was on the verge of firing the nurse, but she bit her lip instead.

The girl slid out of the bed, and into a terrycloth robe. Mildred turned to go back to her own rooms, giving added instructions over her shoulder.

"He might need another feeding now," she said. "But check his milk carefully. One of the bottles surely was spoiled."

"Yes ma'am," the young nurse said, allowing herself a broad smile behind her employer's back. So the little devil had spewed all over her, huh? At least he was capable of something. So far, all she had seen the baby do was sleep and eat. Of course, she had only been there a week.

A moment later she stood looking down into the cradle with one finger pressed to her mouth. The baby was sleeping soundly, face as lovely and as innocent as an angel's, two little fists closed against his cheeks, and the only smell in the cradle was one of baby powder. She put a hand against the blue blanket that covered him, and found it soft and clean and dry. What was with Mrs. Stewart, with rotted milk all over her face and chest? She had given orders to clean up the baby, hadn't she? And yet she must have done it herself? The baby was as sweet and clean as when he was put to bed after his bath late in the afternoon.

It was almost weird how clean he was.

Standing there in the night, with the sound of thunder far away, with the house big and quiet around her, she almost wished ... was beginning to wish she had not taken this job.

# CHAPTER 6

The heat of the late August morning shimmered above the curling blacktop road over the sloping meadow that reached down to the trees along the river. The thick walls and high attic protected the interior of the two-centuries-old house from excessive heat. But the protection was not always welcome. After a few hours of heavy sleep, Felicia always awoke feeling slightly chilled. She got up, opened the window, and felt the warm air surge in upon her.

Far below and to her right the peacock strutted among his hens, striding in and out of the sun and the shadows thrown by a large shade tree. Even farther on a gardener was riding a mower. When she was a kid, she, too, had ridden that mower, pretending it was a car. Sometimes friends had come and joined her. It seemed so long ago, one, or perhaps two, summers past. Long ago, before baby Jeremy.

She dressed quickly in shorts and a sleeveless sweater of knit cotton, and ran along the halls toward the nursery. She always went first to see Jeremy, feeling as though she had been separated from him forever.

This morning a familiar drama was taking place. The young nurse was coming out of her room, a suitcase in each hand. She was wearing a halter dress with long, sloppy skirt, and thong sandals. Her hair was pulled up and held by a rubber band in a kind of untidy ponytail. Felicia had noticed that each nurse was more slovenly than the one before. This one didn't so much as acknowledge her presence. Her face was set and angry. Behind her came Mildred.

"You can't do this! You can't just walk out with no notice whatsoever! It just isn't done that way, Miss — "

"Chantileer! How many times have I had to tell you my name? It's Dorey Chantileer! And yes, ma'am, I *can* leave without notice. You knew when I came here that I'd be working only until my college classes started up. You knew that. So what's the howling about?"

"My dear girl, I was expecting that you would at least stay until the first of September. I have another nurse coming at that time. But that's almost two weeks away."

"I'm sorry. I told you I was sorry, but I have to go now."

"But *why*?" Mildred was almost pleading, and Felicia listened with growing dismay.

Dorey Chantileer turned suddenly on Mildred, bringing her to an abrupt halt. "I'll tell you why! This place is creepy. It's getting to me, you know what I mean? I don't like it here. And I don't see why you need nurses anyway, with all the people around here who aren't doing anything else. Why can't you take care of your own baby, for Pete's sake? You don't have to do another damned thing! You don't even have to mix his formula. My mother raised eight of us, and she was making our living too!" She saw Felicia for the first time, and dropped one suitcase in order to point a finger at her. "And there! What about your other kid? She's always wanting to take care of the baby. Why don't you let her?"

Mildred seemed to draw herself up straighter. Silently she swept round Dorey Chantileer and led the way to the stairs. "I'll call a taxi for you from my office," she said then. "And of course I'll have to write a check for your week's salary. Come along, Dorey."

Dorey shrugged, picked up her suitcase, winked at Felicia and followed Mildred Stewart. Over her shoulder she called, "You don't mind taking care of your little brother for a few days, do you, kid?"

Felicia didn't answer her, nor return her smile. She stood above on the wide balcony, looking down, watching in silence as they descended the stairs. Dorey shrugged again with vague discomfort and embarrassment and fading smile. No matter what she said or did, it was wrong, and she didn't even know what she had said this time. Well, tough. She was glad to be getting out of this house, away from that baby and his people. Not one moment during the week had she felt comfortable.

Felicia turned away, muttering under her breath. "He is not my little brother!"

She went into the nursery and to the cradle. Jeremy was awake and needing attention. His bed and clothing were wet from his heels to his head, and rank with the smell of urine. He most obviously had not been changed this morning. With a moan of sympathy on her lips, she picked him up out of the wetness and the stink and took him into the bathroom, where she laid him, stripped, in the bassinette. She whispered to him as she bathed him, watching with pleasure his beautiful little face, the dimpling in his cheeks as his mouth formed smiles and silent laughters.

"She's gone, and we're glad, aren't we, baby? There's no one to take care of you now but Felicia, and we're so glad, so glad, aren't we, baby? She didn't take good care of you at all. She didn't bathe and change you. But Felicia will. Yes, Felicia will."

She picked him up into a thick towel and, carrying him, went back to pull the soiled blankets from the cradle. She dropped them into the hamper and, working with one hand, tucked a clean sheet into the cradle. It was not smooth, nor straight, but to Felicia this was not an important part of taking care of Jeremy. She brought his clean clothes and sat down in the rocking chair to dress him. His small fingers uncurled and reached for her face, and laughing in delight, she bent forward so that he could reach her cheek and her hair. She pushed her face into the round warmth of his belly and heard him laugh aloud. She opened his hands and pressed them palm-flat against her cheeks, and thought to herself how warm they were now, while at night, when they touched her in the darkness, they were like a touch of icy death. She drew away from him, his hands held firmly in hers, and laid him back upon her knees. His hands were like any baby hands, she was sure, even though she had never really held and looked at any other.

They had perfect little fingers and thumbs, with pink fingernails, and faint lines in the palms, just as there were lines in her own.

Yet his hands were different because they could somehow reach through the walls. Or was it only her memory of them, her desire for them to reach out for her and no one else?

Her mother's voice reached her suddenly, coming nearer and nearer as she talked to someone in the hallway. "It's really very simple, Louise. You give him a bottle every four hours, check him at intervals to see if he needs changing, and just stay near in case he needs you. It's a confining job, but not a difficult one, and it's only or a week or so. The new nurse will be arriving as soon as ... oh, Felicia!"

They had entered the nursery now, Mildred still wearing the cool, flowing caftan of early morning, and close behind her the new downstairs maid.

Louise looked as though she was preparing to walk into the river without knowing how to swim, her pale eyes were wide-set and slightly protuberant, increasing her look of wild-eyed fear. She was in early twenties, and wearing a small engagement ring on her left hand. Felicia knew nothing about her except her name, and she felt fiercely reluctant to turn her baby over to this stranger. All her life, though, she had been cautioned against showing emotions in front of servants.

Mildred's eyes swept the room hastily, from fresh, crooked sheet in the cradle, to a corner of urine-stained blanket sticking out of the hamper. "You cleaned him up, I see," she said, almost accusingly.

"He needed to be cleaned up," Felicia said. "That nurse hadn't cleaned him in hours and hours."

Mildred turned, motioning with her hands, the draped sleeves of the caftan looking like wings fluttering. "Give the baby to Louise, Felicia. She'll take care of him. Come with me, please. I want I talk to you."

Felicia got up, holding the baby close again her breasts, and looked the maid directly in to eyes. Would she feed him and change him and hold him? No, Felicia was sure she wouldn't. She would be like most of the others and leave him in his cradle all the time, lonely and wet and hungry. Felicia nodded her head toward the refrigerator and cabinet.

"His bottle is over there, and you have to warm it up to the correct temperature or he'll get colic. And when you feed him be sure the bottle is tipped so that he doesn't get a lot of air, or he'll get colic. And after he eats, put him face down over your knees or up on your shoulder and burp him and — "

"Felicia!" Mildred's voice was sharp with warning. "I have explained that to Louise. Now please give him to her, and come with me!"

Felicia's lips tightened, and her hold on Jeremy became tightly possessive. She cuddled his body in the crook of her arm, and pressed his head to her cheek. But the night would come, she remembered, and the maid would sleep. She kissed him, but instead of giving him into Louise's arms, she laid him in the cradle. Then with her head high, she followed Mildred from the nursery.

They went downstairs and into the office, a small room with a large desk, ugly uncomfortable straight chairs, and green metal filing cabinets, just off the much larger, comfortable, elegant library. It had been the office in the days long gone when Tanglewood had been a working plantation. Now Mildred wrote the household checks here, dealt with the household accounts, and called members of the staff to account for their deeds. Here they were usually hired and fired, and here too Felicia had always been reprimanded. It was in this room that her pregnancy had been discussed almost a year ago. It was here that her parents had told her they would be getting a divorce.

Felicia hated the office, entered it hesitantly, sensing that no good was to come.

Mildred sat behind the desk and closed her eyes, passing one hand wearily over her face as if it could help clear away her problems. She drew a long breath. "This is getting me down. How I would love a trip away! Perhaps to Europe. If I could only find a nurse I could depend on, I would most certainly go."

Felicia sat forward eagerly. "Mama, you can depend on me! We don't need a nurse. I can take care of him better than anyone else ever could and you could take a trip to Europe. You could start right away. Tomorrow!"

Mildred opened her eyes slowly. "You have got to be crazy! Or do you think I'm crazy? Go off and leave a fourteen-year-old girl in charge not only of a large house and servants but a three-month-old baby too?"

"There's Celta."

"Celta! Don't be absurd. She can't run the house, either!"

Felicia wilted before Mildred's eyes, shrinking into her chair, lower lip trembling faintly. Mildred felt as though both of them would burst into tears the next moment. She pushed away from the desk and went to Felicia and for a few moments held her as she hadn't in so long, as once she had so frequently. Felicia's arms enclosed her waist, and they were silent together. When Mildred moved away, stroking Felicia's soft, shining hair, she felt more capable of facing the present and the future. "I'm sorry, Felicia. I'm being very short tempered lately. I can't for the life of me understand why we can't keep nurses. With you, there was Celta, and only Celta. But that woman has become absolutely adamant against coming upstairs any more. No one wants to work these days. But let's talk of more pleasant things," she said, and put a smile on her face. "Do you remember hearing about Miss Westchester's?"

"You mean the school where you went once?"

"Yes, when I was about your age. I stayed there two years. Until my mother died. Then my grand-mother brought me home, and I've been here ever since, except for my four years at the University. This is the place for Marchants. Grandmother would have been so horrified if she ... but that's impossible to change now, and telling you you made a mistake last summer isn't going to make any difference now. The thing we have to do is correct it."

"Mother," Felicia said, "what are you leading up to?"

"I was telling you about the school. I'm sure you'll love it there, just as I did, and it will put distance between you and motherhood, which is what you need now if we're to carry this out as planned."

"*Mama*! I haven't told anyone that Jeremy is my baby. And I won't, I promise, if you just won't send me away!" She was leaning forward in her chair, anxiety twisting her features. "Why can't I go back in school at Jonesboro?"

"The situation has changed slightly, don't you think? You're no longer the same innocent girl you were last year. I feel another school is warranted now."

"But a girls' school! Mama, why do I have to go to a girls' school?"

"Because I can't trust you any more, Felicia! Did you have to make me say it? I can't trust you with boys!"

"I haven't done anything!"

"Oh don't lie to me, Felicia! You don't get a baby from not doing anything! You're not the Virgin Mary! You are not, nor have you had an immaculate conception! Don't try to deceive me, Felicia.

FELICIA STARED speechless at her mother. She had never seen her so angry. Her fair complexion had turned a dull red, and her chest was rising and failing as though her heart were trying to escape from her body. Felicia sat silent. Now was the time to tell her ... to try to tell her ... that she had been raped that night, but ... by whom? By *what*? Deeply she knew that to bring back the nightmare memories in detail would reveal something that was not human. And she couldn't do that. She wanted to believe that it had never happened. Jeremy had been his own creator. He had planted himself, and he had grown. And she didn't want to leave him.

Mildred pressed her hands to her cheeks briefly as if giving herself courage to carry on. "Felicia, don't make me argue with you. No, that isn't what I intended to say. My goodness, why can't we both just do what we have to do, and not even bother discuss it? You have to go to school. And I have to take care of the baby."

"But it doesn't have to be that way! Why do I need school? Or, why can't I have a tutor? And you ... you don't want to take care of him, and I do. So why should you?"

"Felicia, no! Now I have not only decided about the school, but made the arrangements. They will make room for you. It's a very good school, with strict control, and no bad influences whatsoever, and you certainly don't need to be concerned with the baby anymore. If the nurses persist in leaving unexpectedly, then I or — Louise — will take care of him.

Felicia was looking away, her head turned so far to the right that a cord in her neck was stretched and bulging tightly. She came closer to hating her mother at that moment than she had ever thought possible. The woman sat imperiously behind the large desk, her blond hair a shining crown, her lips thinned and certain of right and wrong. Mildred was sure Felicia had committed a wrong, and she was going to try to eliminate it. And Felicia hated her for it. The golden crown of hair became a self-made halo, and Felicia hated that too.

She turned and looked into her mother's eyes, and saw a kind of pain, and her hatred lessened. So Mildred did not glimpse the fury that had shone in Felicia's eyes.

"When do I have to go?"

"Saturday."

"Will you be taking me?"

"If I can arrange it, I'll drive you up there. It's only two hundred miles. If necessary I can drive up and back in the one day. I'm sure Celta and Louise can manage for one day. Surely."

Felicia felt a stir of hope. "Only two hundred miles? Then I can come home on weekends?"

"For the first month, probably not. After that we'll see," Mildred answered vaguely, and seeing the shadow deepen on Felicia's face, added impulsively, "Since you'll be leaving so soon, why don't you take Jeremy out for a touch of fresh air? Just don't go too far into the woods."

Felicia left the office without looking again at her mother. Her moment of understanding had gone, leaving her lonely and sick with longing. The days, months, years stretched ahead of her endlessly. She was being cast out. And why? What harm had she been doing? She hadn't told anyone that he was hers. She hadn't even talked to anyone other than the nurses, and to them very little. She wouldn't even tell Jeremy, once he was old enough to understand.

She didn't want to leave her mother, either. One year Mildred had gone to Europe for seven weeks and she had stayed here at home with Celta. That had been an oddly lonely time, knowing her mother was so far away. That was the winter she was ten years old.

Nor did she want to leave Tanglewood, with all its familiar corners and quiet, private places, with the terraces behind the house, and the gardens and old barns and stables, the long dark forest rising into the hills and mountains behind the house, the valley and the river in front, and the narrow old road twisting toward town two miles away. She didn't want to leave, but who could she tell except baby Jeremy? A knot of tears had formed in her throat, choking her. She wanted to lay her head down and cry like a baby.

Jeremy would grow, and would no longer know her. And at night, when he reached for her, she would not be there. What would that do to him? Would he too die of loneliness? Or would he just simply forget her?

She entered the nursery to see Louise standing by the windows with her arms folded protectively across her chest. But instead of looking out, she had her back to the light, to the trees beyond the window, and was gazing very intently toward the cradle. She still looked pale and frightened. There was a brightening, a definite glow of relief when Felicia entered the room.

Felicia said, "Is he asleep?"

"I think so." Her arms came down and dangled indecisively at her sides. She seemed awkward, as if not knowing what to do. She said now, "I just left him alone."

"Yes," Felicia bent over the cradle to lift him into her arms. His body contracted, drawing into a ball, and then relaxed against her. "Why don't you go down to the kitchen and mix formula for him while I take him out for a while? It's okay. Mama said I could take him." She paused, seeing the indecision in Louise's face. "You don't have to worry, really. He's very easy to take care of, Louise. There's nothing to be afraid of. You just have to check on him every hour or so, because he doesn't cry, you know. He doesn't expect you to hold him or cuddle him, and absolutely he doesn't want you to talk silly baby talk to him. Just give him his bottle, and it's okay to prop it up, he doesn't mind. And keep him clean. That's all he wants from his nurses."

"Yes, Miss. Thank you. When do you want me to come back upstairs? When will you be bringing him back?"

"I don't know. But Mama will probably want you to be here in just a few minutes. Thirty, maybe."

Felicia took a light blanket in case the air should turn cool, or in case she found a particularly nice place in which Jeremy could lie and watch the leaves and the birds. He was awake now, looking up into her face, his dimples coming with his smile of welcome. Felicia kissed his forehead and, lifting him, hurried out of the nursery and down the front stairs.

She grew suddenly cheerful. The plump baby bounced in her arms, and his mouth opened wide in his delight. A couple of small chuckles escaped, the kind that brought forth Felicia's most youthful giggles. This was a time for play, for they were still together. The sadness would come later.

Mildred, looking out from the office window, saw Felicia running and jumping across the yard with the baby in her arms. She whirled and held him out at arm's length and lifted and lowered him so that he was getting a kind of carnival ride, and even with the distance, Mildred could see the baby was laughing, and Felicia was laughing. But the girl wasn't even watching where she was going. They were near a low brick wall. If they fell, if their heads struck the wall, they could both be killed.

Mildred pounded on the window and called Felicia's name, but the girl kept going, whirling, skipping, bouncing out of view. A moment later they came in view again, passing through a tall hedge and into the back gardens. Now they were walking slowly, the baby held tightly in Felicia's arms, their heads together. Mildred drew a deep breath and reached for the telephone to tell Celta to go after them and bring them back. But then her hand fell away from the phone.

*Let them go. Let them be alone for awhile. They have goodbyes to say.*

Felicia talked to Jeremy as they moved from garden to fountain and finally into the cool shadows of the forest. But not too far. Never too far now, and never toward the top of the hill. She walked more slowly, avoiding the hidden places, the areas of thick growth. Her walks through the summer had made a faint path, and woodland flowers bloomed in the sunny, open places along the way. She explained the flowers the best she knew as to color and species, and pointed to the birds on the wing in the sky. She showed him the moon that was just a pale white crescent in the western sky, and the pine cones on the Austrian Pine. They walked underneath it, and she pinched off a few needles so he could enjoy the fragrance and the feel. His small fingers clutched the pine needles vigorously.

But the ache in her heart was increasing again, and she enclosed the baby in both her arms, holding him closer than he had been since he lay in her womb. And in a way, even more closely than he had been before birth, for now she knew him as a person, as *Jeremy,* and he was more important to her than anyone else in the world. She began whispering to him.

"I didn't want you at first, baby Jeremy, but that was because I didn't know you. I didn't start loving you until after you were born, and now I love you so much it hurts me. I'm being sent away, and I won't see you very often. No more than once a week after school starts. But I don't want you to cry for me, because you must remember that I'll be back. I'll be here to spend all of next summer with you. And I'll be here Thanksgiving and Christmas ... for certain ... maybe between times, on weekends ..."

The tears came, easing from her painfully burning eyes and running slowly down her cheeks to Jeremy's forehead. One of his small hands had taken a clutching hold on her throat, so that he was almost choking her. The other was gripping her hair. It was almost as though he had understood every word she said, but she knew that wasn't possible. He was sensing her anxiety, and was being disturbed by it. For his sake she tried to stop her tears. Her voice halted, swollen in her throat.

She sat down in the cool forest shade and leaned Jeremy back on her raised, bent knees. In her hands she held his small fists, and began to play a little game again, leaning slowly to his face, nose to nose, back and forth until his mouth had opened wide in silent laughter, in delight. And she too began to smile.

Once, as she carried him back among gardens to see the peacock, she thought of just walking on, forever and ever. But fairyland was not available.

She had an Uncle Martin somewhere in the world, in New York, she thought. But he was her mother's brother, and would never go against his sister's wishes. She had a father, too, but he had demanded an abortion long before Jeremy was born. He hadn't even wanted the baby to be born at all. And at least her mother had cared enough to see him born.

And now she cared enough to keep him in her home, where he would be warm and fed.

It was Felicia she was sending away.

# CHAPTER 7

Felicia's bags were packed and ready for the trip in the morning. She sat on the foot of her bed, her legs drawn up, and stared blindly out the west window. The sun had gone below the dark treetops, leaving brilliant streaks of color in the sky that ranged from soft pink to deep orange. But the colors blurred, as did the shape of trees, and the slope of valley. Her room was deeply shadowed now, and very quiet. Felicia was tired, even though she had taken a nap in the afternoon when Jeremy was sleeping. She hadn't slept well these past two nights, since she had learned she was being sent away. Jeremy too had seemed restless, his small hands groping, touching her, rousing her from sleep, gripping her more tightly than usual. Was he aware that she was leaving, or was he growing stronger?

Felicia lay down, her arms curved for a pillow, her knees drawn tightly up. It was almost time for dinner, but she was so tired. Her eyes drooped shut, and the dwindling light faded completely.

She fell into a deep sleep as soft as a black cloud, floating her body gently, easing her exhaustion. The tiny, cold fingers touched her arm. She came partly awake, aware of the touch, but too tired to move. The fingers tightened, pinching, harder and harder, until the pain roused her and she sat up to find the light had gone completely from her room. With one hand she caressed her arm, rubbing the stinging flesh. Unwillingly she glanced behind her, and shrank back against the headboard.

*Where was he*?

Did she really want to see him, here in her room, capable of hurting her now?

*No. Oh no.*

Why did she feel so afraid when she knew he was calling her because he wanted her? Why was she afraid at all, when she loved him so much?

She slid off her bed, ran to the closet, grabbed her favorite sweater and left her room, pulling the sweater on as she hurried through dark halls.

She went first to the nursery, as she always did. The doors stood open, from hallway to nurse's room, from hallway to nursery. No one was in the nurse's room. Nor was anyone in the nursery except Jeremy.

Her fear dissipated when she looked down at him. He was an angel, this baby of hers, sleeping soundly and deeply, lying on his back, his small head turned slightly to one side so that his fist poked into one cheek and made it look fatter and rounder than the other. He drew a long sigh when she picked him up, and his body, limp at first, drew into a small knot that she hugged with overwhelming love.

*Of course he hadn't been in her room, not tonight or ever. Her mother was right, it was only a dream. A strange, recurring dream.*

She held him only a moment, then put him back into the cradle. She bent and kissed him, and still he slept, undisturbed.

Louise came quietly into the room, stopping several feet away.

"Celta said to tell you they're waiting dinner on you."

Felicia gave the baby a final, gentle touch. "I'm on my way," she said. "I just stopped by to see how Jeremy is."

"He's no trouble at all. He's a lot easier to take care of than I was afraid he'd be. Of course I do like you said, I just change him and feed him. I don't mind it at all." She added as Felicia was leaving the room, "The worst thing is just staying up here all the time so he won't be alone. That's the worst part."

"You could read," Felicia said. "There are hundreds of books in the library. Many are novels."

Felicia glanced back from the doorway. Louise was gazing at the cradle with a look of concentration that came close to being a frown.

THEY ATE in the small informal breakfast room, just the two of them. It had been that way most of Felicia's life. On those occasions when her father was home, they had sometimes eaten in the large, formal dining room, but most of the time there were dinner parties there, or away from home, which her mother and father attended without her. Then, she ate in the kitchen with Celta, and liked it that way. Celta told her old stories of her own childhood, of Ireland and Scotland. She told her fairy tales, and stories of the little people, the gnomes, the elves, all those who lived in tiny homes among the huge, fat, swollen tree roots deep in the woods and forests.

She told her of the changelings.

Mildred did not tell stories. She talked instead of current issues, touching on politics, the arts, science. Or her travels and experiences. But for several months Mildred hadn't even gone to the country club, a necessary deprivation if she were to pass herself off as having another baby. She rarely gossiped about her acquaintances. She was, Felicia thought, not nearly so interesting as Celta.

Mildred's conversation tonight was almost nonexistent, as though she too were tired and thoughtful. She stared down the table past Felicia, and lighted a cigarette long before dessert came. And when dessert finally came, she turned it down in favor of a cocktail. Felicia ate her dessert in silence.

Felicia caught Mildred's eyes on her, drifting slowly from her hair to her shoulder. "You're wearing your sweater?" Mildred asked, as if she couldn't believe what she was seeing. "It's much too warm for a sweater. Take it off."

She obeyed without comment and hung the sweater over one post of her chair. It wasn't really that chilly.

"Felicia, what's wrong with your arm?"

Felicia looked down. Two small marks stood out brutally red against her naturally pale skin, and others were already turning blue. They were easily counted, in two groups of five; four tiny fingertips and one thumb, bunched, as though they had tried to penetrate her skin.

Felicia covered them with her palm. "I guess it's mosquito bites," she said, wishing she hadn't taken her sweater off. She did not want her mother to see, she herself did not want to see the marks. On touching now, she found that the entire area around the bruises was sore.

"Mosquitoes! Why didn't you tell me you had mosquitoes in your room? We could have had it fogged." She had risen from her chair and was coming to look. Her hand clasped Felicia's wrist and pulled it closer. "Those aren't bites, Felicia, they're bruises. What happened?"

"I don't know," Felicia said. She was not lying, she was telling the truth as her mother would understand it, as she herself understood it. She knew only that she had felt the hands, the intense pressure, the pain. She hoped her mother wouldn't ask her any more questions.

"You must have struck your arm against something. The way you've been going through the halls at night, I'm not surprised that you bump into things now and then." Mildred was moving away, back to her own chair. "Do you have your things packed and ready to go? We'll be leaving early tomorrow morning. I'm going to drive you, and we'll have lunch in the city and do some shopping. Would you like that?"

"Yes, Mama. May I be excused now? I want to wash my hair."

Mildred nodded and sighed. She had suspected, she had feared, that Felicia would refuse to leave, and if she did there would be nothing Mildred could do but accept her decision. That is, short of forcibly ejecting her. But so far it seemed that Felicia hadn't thought of refusing to leave, and was obeying her in getting ready to go, in going. But the hours dragged. Nine o'clock was moving toward ten very slowly. It was still twelve more hours before she could safely load Felicia and her luggage into the car and drive away.

Thank God Jeremy wasn't old enough to cry after her or miss her.

Once Felicia was in school the decision to go or not to go would not so easily be changed. Without money for fare home, she would have to stay at Miss Westchester's. Until Mildred could talk with her, reason with her, convince her.

She felt an unwelcome twinge of guilt, and a deep, aching surge of loneliness. It was not too late to change her mind and keep Felicia with her, to send her on the local school bus to Jonesboro Junior High. As before, she could come running home at night filled with news about school, with eyes as bright as stars. But no, that had ended several long months ago.

She had to send Felicia away, for her own good.

BEFORE SHE WENT on to her room, Felicia sat with Jeremy for a while rocking his cradle, staring down at him, engraving upon her memory every line of his face, every fleeting dimple; the perfect beauty which he possessed. He slept soundly the whole time she gazed at him, his pink lips moving occasionally in dream suckling, and sometimes twitching into a brief smile.

She went to her room and shampooed her hair and blow-dried it, so that it was like flying threads of silk. She spent a while playing with dryer and hair, making the hair lift and dance and fly. She pointed the nozzle of the dryer to other interesting areas, under her arms, between her breasts, down her body, flattening her pajamas against her, billowing them like banners waving in the wind. She giggled, and for a moment unhappiness belonged to yesterday and tomorrow.

And she remembered to pack the dryer also. One of the last-minute things she had to do. And her room became very quiet and filled with ghosts with the swooshing noise of the blower stilled.

It was close to midnight when she climbed into bed and turned out her light. She was sleepy, and her pillow was soft and clean, and the light-weight blanket just enough to ward off the chill night air that came through her raised window.

The hand touched her cheek, so cold that chills radiated from it and caused her to curl closer into her blanket. The little hand lay still on her forehead, moved down onto her cheek again and across her mouth, lingering there for a moment. When it began to pat her cheek she opened her eyes, her breath stilled, her heart pounding. Her eyes turned cautiously toward the door. The faint starlight that came through her windows touched upon the door just enough for her to see that it was closed, locked as she had left it.

She had forgotten to leave her light on.

The pats were getting harder, faster and faster, so that her cheek began to sting. She drew sharply sideways, and whispered, "Please don't do that!" But the touching came with her, moving with her movement, and was now painful, slapping, urgent, crying out for attention. She rolled to her side and reached for the lamp, and her hand struck the base and knocked it off the table. The slaps on her cheeks, now on both sides as though he stood directly above her and was trying with growing strength to direct her attention his way, were so fiery and painful that her eyes were filling with tears. She leaned over the side of the bed and reached for the lamp with one hand, while with the other she reached to grasp his hands and hold them.

"*No! No, Jeremy!*"

But there was nothing of substance to hold. Her face burned and stung and the slaps continued, and she found the lamp and pulled it up, sobs breaking at last from her throat. Her fingers touched the switch, and the moment the light came on the slaps abruptly stopped.

For a few minutes she sat on the side of her bed and leaned her face into her hands. The tears that dropped between her fingers were born of pain, of fear, of sorrow. Her whispers were muffled against the palms of her hands. "*What do you want of me? Why are you hurting me*?

She left her room, but not in darkness. She turned on lights as she went, leaving a trail of brightness behind her as she passed from hallway to hallway and finally to the door of the nursery. She approached his cradle with more caution and watchfulness than ever before, but the moment she saw him all that was forgotten. He was three and a half months of round little baby boy, and his deep blue eyes were watching steadily over the side of his cradle for her, and the moment she came in sight his mouth opened wide in the mirthful, toothless smile she loved.

She picked him up and held him out from her and his plump little hands reached and flexed, and the grin, the soundless laughter, the delight in his eyes grew mischievous and impishly playful. She responded with a soft giggle. The nursery was quiet and dimly lighted, and the grandfather clock downstairs resoundingly struck the hour of one-thirty. Her voice was a hissing whisper.

"You precious ... *you little imp. You devil.*"

The delight sparkled in his eyes, and his hands, unable to reach her, came back in fists to fill his mouth, one slipping out as the other slipped in, both soft and almost formless, like twin balls of pink flesh and tender appendages. *But they could hurt so much, so much …*

She drew him close into her arms, under her chin, against her breast, and felt the willing pliability of his response. Confusion tore into her emotions. Her baby was so sweet, so perfect. The other was only a bad dream, a terrible nightmare.

"No, I'm sorry, my precious," she whispered against the top of his head. "I didn't mean it when I called you an imp and a devil. You're not. You're my little boy. Mine."

She warmed his bottle and gave it to him, and he nursed greedily, emptying it faster and faster each time she fed him it seemed, gazing steadily up into her face the whole while as though he too were absorbing all that she was, just as she impressed his image upon a memory that would never end.

He fell asleep in her arms, but she couldn't give him up. She rocked slowly and he sighed and slept ever more deeply. She drew her legs up into the rocking chair, knees leaning against wooden arms, and made a warm cradle for him in the curve of her belly and thigh, pillowing his head in the crook of her arm. She too slept, dozing lightly, falling at last into a deep, timeless sleep.

Her mother woke her long past daybreak. Sunshine touched the window sill, glinted on the clean nursery windows. Felicia jerked nervously at the hand on her shoulder, and saw her mother standing over her, and Louise a few feet away.

"Have you been here all night?" Mildred asked in amazement.

Felicia straightened cramped legs and arms and looked down into Jeremy's face. He was chewing on a fist hungrily, his eyes following the movement of the leaves outside the window as they danced in the gusting summer wind. He was warmly wet, right through to her pajamas and skin.

Mildred didn't wait for an answer from Felicia. She said, "Take the baby, Louise. And you, Felicia, hurry and shower and dress. We must get started if we're going to do any shopping at all."

Felicia realized that the time had come. She had to say goodbye to her baby now, and when she saw him again he would no longer be her baby, but her mother's. As Louise reached for him, Felicia kissed his cheek, and then, before the threat of tears burst into reality, she ran from the room.

THE TRIP TO WASHINGTON, D.C., was mostly silent. The Mercedes glided smoothly along under Mildred's hands, covering the miles at the speed limit. They lunched at Le Bagatelle early in the afternoon before spending the remainder of the afternoon shopping. But Felicia could not easily pretend to enjoy herself. The new clothes were as nothing in the emptiness of her heart. When at last they drew up on the quiet, tree-lined street in front of the red brick four-story building, Felicia felt that if she had to speak she would burst into tears that would never stop. Mildred was forcing brightness, but Felicia saw her desire to be on her way through the open country in her car.

In the office Felicia was introduced to Miss Aldrich, a very neat lady with a trim hair style and only the merest suggestion of makeup. Felicia sat stiffly while her mother and Miss Aldrich exchanged a few comments about school of today and yesterday. Felicia heard her mother say she had loved it here, and she was sure her daughter would love it also. Felicia, tense with emotion she dare not show, looked at the credentials on the wall in their walnut frames, at the stark draperies on the window. Nowhere else in the building was there a sound. She realized Miss Aldrich was talking to her, smiling professionally.

"I beg your pardon?" Felicia said softly. "I'm sorry ..."

"Your roommate," Miss Aldrich repeated, "has gone for the weekend. She'll return tomorrow afternoon. Her name is Sherrie, and she's very close to your age. I'm sure you'll like each other."

Felicia swallowed the knot in her throat, but it remained with her, growing solidly. She longed to go into her room and remain there, hidden. She was glad Sherrie was gone. "Yes, ma'am," she said finally. "I'm sure we will."

Miss Aldrich pressed a buzzer on her desk; a man in work clothes appeared and was sent after the luggage and the boxes of new clothes. Felicia and Mildred followed Miss Aldrich up the long, sturdy stairway to the third floor, where the headmistress opened a door upon a quite small, very simple room. It had one window, long and deep, and two narrow beds. It was two bedrooms in one, separated by an invisible line down the center.

"Felicia, you may sleep late tomorrow. I trust you'll sleep well," Miss Aldrich said.

"Thank you, ma'am," Felicia said.

Mildred hugged and kissed her and said, "You'll like it here, Felicia, after you get used to it. Remember, I came here once also, and I know how you're feeling." Her voice had lowered so that it obviously was meant only for Felicia's ears, and Miss Aldrich, smiling nearby, pretended not to hear.

Felicia swallowed again, and nodded. Then she threw her arms around her mother's shoulders and clung to her until Mildred began pushing against the embrace lightly but definitely. Felicia didn't have to look to see that Mildred had tears on her cheeks. They had dampened her own cheeks.

"I must go," Mildred said softly. "Even now it will be very late when I get home. Goodbye, dear."

"Bye, Mama." Felicia turned her back to them and kept her head lowered until they and the handyman had gone out and closed the door behind them. Their footsteps echoed in the uncarpeted hall. Felicia sank down onto the cool floor, feeling unfamiliar polished wood against her legs.

At midnight Mildred pulled over in front of an all-night convenience store in Jonesboro. She was only a few miles from home now, and felt she could safely take a break. She walked on trembling legs into the bright lights of the store and bought a soft drink that was high in caffeine. The girl behind the counter was only about sixteen, not familiar to her except that she reminded her for a moment of Felicia. She wondered if they were friends, but decided not. The girl who waited on her was probably two years older, two grades ahead of Felicia.

She returned to her chair and sat for several minutes smoking a cigarette, sipping her drink, and staring into the darkness beyond the lights of the store. Her brain felt numb with tiredness. She wished only to get home and into bed, and she hoped fervently that Louise would not need her.

She started the car and drove through deserted streets to the road that wound its way along the edge of the valley toward Tanglewood. It was a beautiful drive, a tunnel of green in the summer, and sometimes a tunnel of white in the winter, with long icicles hanging from the bluffs, and every twig expanded three times its size with moist,clinging snow. Tonight the green was nearly black in the lights of the car, with tree trunks rearing suddenly into the lights, and passing by to be replaced by others. The road curved left and right, out of one twist into another, so that speed limit signs were scarcely necessary. Few drivers could handle more than forty miles an hour and stay out of the trees. Mildred didn't mind the unfolding curves. It was a familiar drive, and a great relief from the heavy traffic of the interstate. She kept the lights on dim, for brights overshot the narrow road and were lost among the trees.

The tires squealed on a sharp curve, and the lights picked up the gray-black of a bluff and swept on to a large tree trunk that reached within inches of the road, and a flash of something in the center of the road caught her attention. She glanced to the side, her hands light on the wheel, but saw nothing beyond the darkness, the gray trunks, the dip of the hillside toward the valley, lost now in the night. She didn't have time to put on the brake, to slow the car, before she saw it again, and this time, hanging directly over the hood of her car, half-lighted by the glare of her lights so that it seemed a ghoulish specter from some

Halloween surprise party, sprung perhaps from an opened box, an almost invisible blue tail writhing and curling, propelling it into the air, pointing toward her a tiny twisted face with darting tongue and cold, flat eyes ... and yet there were hands growing from a half materialized body, reaching toward her, fingers hooked and claw-like, reaching into her windshield ...

*Jeremy.*

She screamed. She thought she screamed, but the sound was only part of the rest of the horror, of her jerk on the steering wheel to avoid the body of the thing, and of the crash off the left side of the road into a tree that stopped the car from plunging downhill toward the river. There was the sound of metal smashing, crumpling, of the engine roaring, of the horn in the night, and then silence, and darkness. Total, unrelieved darkness.

The steering wheel pressed hard into her stomach, shoved back as it was almost to the seat. She sobbed softly, her hands covering her eyes, then pushing her hair back. She sobbed from fear, not pain, fear of what she had seen, not of the accident.

She opened her eyes and held her breath. The insects of the night and the birds, the whippoorwills, the owls, had silenced. The only sound now was the easing of metal, one bit against another as the car leaned farther over the side of the road and downhill. She was afraid to move. Afraid not of unbalancing the car, not that the car might find a way between the trees, to fall over a bluff a hundred feet or more — but afraid of what she had seen, as though a movement might bring it back again.

*But what had she seen?*

Of course it was nothing but a hallucination, caused by exhaustion, and the long months of emotional stress. What had been only in her own mind could not possibly hurt her if she faced its origin. Therefore, she should get out of the car, carefully but quickly, and walk on home. The darkness along the road was no worse than the darkness here.

She sucked her breath in, flattening her diaphragm even more, and struggled out from between the wheel and the seat. Her handbag was on the seat in her way, and she clutched its leather strap in her hand. She moved uphill, toward the passenger door. She found the door handle and with effort managed to push it open far enough to slip through. She found, when her feet touched the sloping ground, that she had lost one shoe somewhere back in the car. She removed the other one, found the pavement, and turned towards home, the night intensely black around her. Fear tugged at her back like tiny fingers plucking ... like the fingers she had seen glowing in the lights of the car for that second before the crash.

She thought of Jeremy's first nurse, Janet Duncan, who had died so horribly somewhere along this road, perhaps exactly here where she now walked. If Janet Duncan's murderer had ever been found, Mildred did not know of it. Could he still be here somewhere, perhaps hidden in the network of small caves scattered through the area? But they were said to be too small for a man. But could it have been the murderer, hidden somewhere in the area, who had thrown something in front of her car? To frighten her. To stop her ... so that he ... could ... but, Jeremy's face ... Jeremy's hands reaching for her ...

*Hallucination*, she reminded herself sternly, her own mind had created the picture.

She began to run nevertheless, faster and faster, blind in the dark, her feet slapping against the pavement, a sound as foreign and alien as that which pushed her on and on in her efforts to escape whatever it was that reached for her. Other sounds seemed to be following her, on the upper side of the road, on the rise of the hill. Rustlings, slitherings in the leaves, across the stones at the mouths of the little caves, and another thought formed in her mind. Snakes will crawl onto a road at night because it has retained the heat of the day. *God ... what if she stepped on one*? She remembered a time long ago, when she was still a small child, there had been an infestation of snakes along this road, over the valley and down on the river. A herpetologist had come to study the reptiles, to try to discover the reason for their sudden appearance, to find out where they had come from and where they were going, and how they could be destroyed. It was a species he did not recognize, appearing to be a mutation, and in trying to capture some of them he had found them excessively aggressive and poisonous as vipers. People were warned to stay away from them. She could remember clearly now her nightmares concerning those snakes; she could see them in the darkness, writhing bodies, tangling together, too numerous to count, covering the road, the hillside They had seemed to be migrating toward the hill or coming out of it, for some purpose of their own. She had begun to fear the woodland from that time. And at dusk, or in the dark, they were so hard to see. For three weeks they had seemed to be everywhere, and then one morning they were gone. At last the herpetologist decided they had gone into the hill, into the hundreds of caves that opened beneath the small bluffs all along the side of the hill to the very top, and the only way to destroy them would be to destroy the hill, and that was impossible. Anyway, they were gone, and gradually, over the years, they had been forgotten.

She remembered them now. As though the apparition she had seen brought them to mind. Half-serpent, half-human. And the most horrible part was that her mind had created it in the image of her own grandchild.

What was wrong with her? Was she beginning to need psychiatric help?

She came out of the shadow of trees sooner than she expected and saw faint starlight outlining the wings and chimneys of Tanglewood. Still it seemed far away, the circle drive past the pillar of the entrance going on and on. Her feet were raw and burning, her stockings destroyed from the rough paving. But she kept running, pushed on by unwanted fears and warnings deep in her own psyche. Not until she had climbed the steps and entered the dimly lighted hall did she pause, take a look at herself in the closest mirror, and smile at her foolishness. Her hair looked as though it belonged to a witch. Her face had bright red cheeks. Her stockings were nothing but ladders of runs. She was glad that no one had seen her wild flight through the dark night as though demons flew at her shoulders.

She went cautiously upstairs and into her room, but on her way into the bath she paused and turned. The carpet was soft and deep, but still the pain in her feet seemed to increase as she went slowly into the nursery. It was so quiet here, as though the cradle was empty, as though she had not imagined what she had seen in the glare of her headlights, as though he somehow had ...

From several feet away, she looked down into the cradle. There was the round bulge of the blue blanket, just as always. She stepped closer, the hair on the back of her neck and along her arms rising in primitive warning, preparing her for something she had never faced before. But then she let out her breath in a great, long sigh, and smiled. For there he was, just as she must have known he would be, fast asleep, wrapped in innocence found only in the helpless infant.

# CHAPTER 8

Felicia lay in the narrow, unfamiliar bed and stared at the ceiling. Sometimes she turned her head and looked at the small clock on her bedside table, but then she went back to staring at the ceiling. The bright room light was on, leaving no corner of the room in shadow. The other bed was still empty. Her thoughts dwelled for a moment on the girl who would be coming tomorrow, but only for a moment.

She looked at the clock again. Two-forty-five. Mama would be home by now, asleep in her bed. Louise too would be sleeping. There was no one to go to Jeremy and give him his two o'clock bottle, now that she was gone, and she could feel his need, his loneliness and confusion, more even than she felt her own. His were fed by lack of understanding. He could not know where she was, why she did not come to him, why her room was silent and empty. He would not cry, she knew, he would simply lie there waiting for her. Would he soon feel deserted by her? He could not know how her heart was a nucleus of pain ... and yet, she had not turned out her light so that he could reach her, if he could, at this distance, in this strange place.

*It isn't true, like Mama had said, that it was only a dream. It was something crazy that happened to my mind when I was pregnant. Things like that aren't possible for tiny babies like Jeremy, nor for anyone, even the magicians like the one I saw in Venus that time. The magician waved his arms slowly with his cloak falling away like the wings of bats, and the prone girl rose into the air a bit at a time while I held my breath, while all the audience held its breath, until she was lying in the air several inches above the table, but they said afterwards that it was all an act, that those things couldn't really happen. Daddy was almost angry that I believed it. But I didn't really believe it, not with all my mind, just part of it. The bruises on my arm don't really prove anything. I don't want to believe that he can ... and yet I do ... but I'm afraid ... because I don't understand ...*

THE BRIGHT LIGHT above gave her double vision when she looked away and closed her eyes — two bright balls of light bouncing against her eyelids. It was silly to leave the light on, especially the one in the ceiling, but she couldn't make herself get up and go to the switch that controlled it. Instead, she pulled up the cover and hid her head beneath it, and finally the reflection of the light stopped bouncing in her closed eyes.

She woke with a faint sense of wonder: it was morning. In fact, it was nearly eleven. She had not been awakened once. He had not found her. Her thoughts instantly went home to the nursery. The sun would be shining there on the floor, making bright trails toward his cradle, and Louise would be up and seeing about him, bathing him, feeding him, and he wouldn't be so lonesome, even though he didn't like her. Sleep had drawn a film over her own loneliness, so that she began to wonder how it would be here. No boys to pass notes to down the row of seats, nor to receive notes from. Gary Appleby — the boy with the red hair and freckles at Jonesboro Junior High — would be passing notes to someone else this year, probably, just as he probably had the last semester of last year. Not that she cared. Gary Appleby was a creepy crawler anyway. Still, it would seem rather odd not to have notes coming her way, all folded into a grimy little wad as if to make themselves invisible from the teacher. Would her friends miss her, or had they already forgotten about her?

She showered, shampooed her hair, and dried it. It fell over her shoulders and down her back, soft and separating in her fingers.

AT NOON SOMEONE knocked on her door. She opened it to see Miss Aldrich smiling. She wore her smile just as she wore her hair and the gold chain at her throat, as part of her professional costume. Felicia had a smile of her own available on shortest notice, a trick learned long ago from her mother.

"Felicia, how are you today?"

"Very well, thank you, Ma'am. Won't you come in?"

"I would prefer that you come downstairs now, Felicia, for lunch. You're surely ready to eat something, since you skipped breakfast."

"Yes, Ma'am," Felicia answered without interest. Sounds came from below and from along the hall, sounds that she had not heard inside her room. Giggles. Muted voices. The throb and pulse of a school.

As they walked downstairs to the dining room Miss Aldrich said, "On Saturday and Sunday mornings we allow our girls to sleep late if they wish, and go without breakfast if that is what they desire, or eat later than usual, but only on weekends. Every school day precisely at seven in the morning a bell will ring, and you'll have thirty minutes to get ready and be down for breakfast. Classes begin at eight-thirty."

"Yes, Ma'am."

They began to pass groups of girls who paid them little attention other than polite hellos, and Miss Aldrich continued to talk softly as she walked beside Felicia. They reached open double doors at the end of a long hall, and Miss Aldrich stopped.

"This is the cafeteria, Felicia. You can sit where you wish, mingle and enjoy yourself. Your roommate will be here sometime this afternoon. If there is anything you want, don't hesitate to ask me. I'm either always in the office or available to the office."

"There is something, Miss Aldrich. Am I permitted to call home whenever I want?"

"Of course you are, within reason. There are no room phones for obvious reasons, but there is a phone in the downstairs lobby, and if your parents don't object, it's yours to use as you feel the need." Miss

Aldrich touched Felicia's arm as though to show affection and sympathy, but the professional smile didn't alter. "And now I have other business. Have a good day, dear."

Felicia moved hesitantly into the cafeteria, drawn by the odors of food and the emptiness of her stomach, but she had never felt so alone in her life. All the girls around her knew one another, it seemed, and were delighted to meet again after a long summer. None of them noticed her now that Miss Aldrich was no longer with her.

At the end of the glass counter, she picked up a tray and silverware wrapped in a blue and white checked napkin and moved along with the growing line of girls to choose food displayed on ice or steam tables. Balancing her tray against sudden turns by laughing girls ahead of her, Felicia made her way to a corner table where she sat alone. She hurried with her eating, taking only a few bites to ease the hunger. Now that she knew she could call home, she was anxious to do so. She returned her tray to a table near the counters as she saw others doing, and went in search of the telephone.

The lobby was to the left of the entrance, a kind of family room with tables and chairs and scattered magazines and games. In one corner sat a television. An old movie was playing to no audience that Felicia saw. The telephone hung on the wall near the door, and Felicia placed a collect call to her mother.

The familiar voice answered, questioningly, accepting the call, and Felicia felt weak with gladness.

"Felicia, is something wrong?" her mother asked immediately, her voice lifting as it did when she was worried.

"No, Mama, I'm okay. I was just wondering about Jeremy and everything. Is he all right, Mama?"

"Of course he's all right, Felicia. Did you think he wouldn't be? Louise is taking very good care of him, I'm pleased to say. She even seems to enjoy it."

"Did she give him his feeding in the night? Like I always did?"

"I'm sure she must have. At any rate, he isn't starving. Has your new roommate come in yet?"

"No."

"When she does you'll begin to enjoy yourself more, I'm sure. I do wish you'd try, dear, and keep your mind free of concern as much as possible and try to make up for lost months at school."

"Mother, I will. I promise. I don't mind it as much today as I did last night, really. But I wanted to call home. You didn't have trouble on the road, I guess."

"Oh my! I got almost home and totally wrecked my car and had to walk the rest of the way in complete darkness. I tore the bottom out of my hose because one of my shoes was lost so I threw the other away, and today I'm mostly just sitting here giving the bottom of my feet a chance to heal." She ended with a feeble burst of laughter.

Felicia tried to absorb the scene her mother had painted, that completely unbelievable picture of her mother going barefoot down the road in the dark of the night, with her car left somewhere behind in a crumpled mess.

"Mama! What happened?"

There was a slight hesitation, then Mildred said, "I must have gotten too tired. I thought I saw something in front of the car and it startled me, and the next thing I knew I was going over the side toward the lake and straight into the trees."

"And you weren't hurt?"

"Only my pride, and my feet. From the pavement. I had never realized how rough that road is before. Those tiny rocks in that macadam are like needles. But I made it, and it's rather amusing from other angles I suppose. I'm sure the garage man who came out with his wrecker was amused, even though he tried to look very serious. Or maybe it's my own sense of the ridiculous, because he did say I was lucky to have gotten out alive. If I'd been fatter than I am the steering wheel would have crushed me, he said. But I really had no trouble getting out of the car and on home."

"Mama, I'm sorry."

"Oh, I am home safely, and the only loss is mechanical."

"You said you saw something in the road?"

"Not really. It was just my exhaustion and nervousness, I'm sure. I was probably driving faster than I thought, also. Certainly it's nothing for you to worry about. Run along now and get acquainted with some of the girls, and have a good time."

"Yes, Mama." Anxiously, before her mother could hang up, Felicia cried, "Mama? Would you be sure to give Jeremy his two o'clock feeding?" Another hesitation. Felicia heard her mother draw a long breath.

"Felicia," Mildred said carefully, "I want you to stop worrying about the baby. He's fine. If he wakes and wants a bottle during the night, he shall have one."

"But you won't know if he's awake if you don't check on him."

"I'm sure if he were that desperate he'd let someone know, Felicia. Babies can make themselves heard."

"But Jeremy doesn't cry. And he likes to be held in the night, Mama."

"I'm sure all of this is in your imagination, Felicia, but if it will make you less anxious and worried I most certainly will see to it that he is fed and held during the night. Now, goodbye, dear."

"*Wait*, Mama. Are you coming after me next weekend?"

"No, dear, not that soon. You need to get used to being away from home first. Goodbye, Felicia. I'll call you in a few days."

Felicia hung up the phone, feeling trapped. She found a deep leather chair with ottoman and sank into it and stared at the distant, angled television screen until it blurred into a cauldron of colors and moving figures. She flipped through a magazine. Finally, she got up and went back upstairs to her room.

She found the door standing open and suitcases in the middle of the floor. The closet door on the far side of the room was also open, and a slender, small girl backed out of it and turned to face her, eyes widening in startled surprise. But the look was immediately gone and replaced by a smile.

"Hello."

It was a half-shy greeting, friendship tentatively offered but subject to quick withdrawal. Felicia observed the girl in one all-over glance. She was pretty in an average way, with light brown hair and brown eyes. Her hair was drawn back behind her ears. She was wearing jeans and loose checked blouse.

"I'm Felicia Stewart." The girl's smile widened a bit and her head nodded, but her eyes reflected questions. Felicia added, "This is my room, too. Miss Aldrich said I'd have a roommate named Sherrie. I thought maybe that's who you are?"

"Oh! Sure! I'm Sherrie. Nobody told me about you. But I just got in, so I guess nobody had a chance, right? Well, it's great to see you, Felicia. I hope you don't mind having a roommate."

"Oh, no. At least I don't think I do. I've never had one before."

Sherrie went on about her business, hanging things in the closet and folding others into drawers. Her movements were quick and energetic and she talked in a nonstop stream, it seemed to Felicia.

"I've had lots of roommates, and I love it, but I don't get nearly as much homework done because I would much rather talk and listen to music if I've got someone to play with — you know what I mean — a friend who enjoys the same things I do.

Of course I'm open to suggestions, and if I have a quiet roommate, that's all right too, I don't mind. I brought my record player, but we're really not supposed to, and we most certainly aren't allowed to play it loud enough to be heard in the hall. Did you know there's a kind of sentry that patrols the hall every so often all day and night? There is!" She leaned toward Felicia for a moment of conspiratorial whispering before she went back to unpacking. "It varies who it is, I think, but anyway, they always know who still has a light on after ten and who is playing records or radio too loud! We call them spies. Our lights have to be out by ten, you know. My last roommate left at the end of last semester. We correspond. When did you get here? What grade are you in?"

Felicia answered the last question first, just in case. "The ninth."

"Oh really? Is that all? Somehow I thought you were older. How old are you?"

"Fourteen."

Sherrie's eyes swept Felicia from head to feet. She sat on the floor on her knees and heels, her head lowered slightly as she drew the last items from her suitcase. "You look older," she said. "I thought when I first saw you that you were probably a sophomore at least, but I'm glad you're just my age. That always makes it nice. Have you met many of the girls?"

Sherrie's vivaciousness carried over into the afternoon and evening, pulling Felicia along, making the time move faster and faster until Felicia found herself not minding Miss West-Chester's at all. Sherrie introduced her to so many girls Felicia couldn't remember half the names.

The unfamiliar situation became uncomfortable again when it was time for bed, and Sherrie stripped without self-consciousness and left the bathroom door open as she showered and pulled on pajamas.

"You can go ahead, Felicia, and use the tub if you want," she called out as she leaned over the wash basin to brush her teeth, baggy pajamas drooping off her narrow bottom, her bare feet flat on the floor. "I'll only be a minute more."

"I'll wait. I don't mind," Felicia answered.

"Oh, I know, you're not used to sharing your bathroom, right? Well, you'll get used to it. Me, I've been in boarding schools ever since I was six years old."

Felicia waited until Sherrie had flopped onto her bed, and then she very carefully closed the bathroom door. The mirror showed her a body far more mature than Sherrie's, a body that revealed her recent pregnancy in fuller, darker nipples, and a slightly darker line of skin running down from her navel. Would Sherrie look at her and know there was a baby somewhere? Would she want Sherrie to know? No. Never. It was like being two different people, like having a secret dream, a secret she could never share with anyone. She could say to Sherrie, "I have a little brother ..." But saying it like that, even thinking it, gave her a feeling of disloyalty to her baby, *and he was her baby*, even though her mother wished he weren't. It would be easier not to mention him at all than to say something that was untrue and disloyal. When Sherrie and the other girls were talking to her it was easier to be a girl again, but when the voices ceased, her heart began its silent reminders that she was someone different now.

When she left the bathroom Sherrie had turned out her bedside lamp, and spoke sleepily from her shadowed corner. "We can't keep lights on, Felicia. Don't forget to turn out the bathroom light."

Felicia felt a moment of panic. "But ..." she said, confused, undecided, "I kept lights on last night. No one said anything."

"That's because it was your first night. If there's a light on after ten they'll come in and turn it out because you're supposed to sleep, and if you have a light on they'll figure you're reading comic books or something."

Felicia returned to the bathroom and snapped off the light. There was no more sound from Sherrie's corner of the room, and Felicia sat in bed a moment, her hand on the switch of her table lamp. At last she gave it the slight twist that removed all light from the room, and she slid down into bed and pulled up the light blanket and held it tight.

It was the first of many nights in which relaxation would be slow to come. But gradually she almost forgot that she had ever feared the dark, or dreaded the night. And indeed there was no need to.

Not for three weeks.

At first it was just a suggestion of having been touched that woke Sherrie, like the lingering half-memory of a dream. She lay still for a moment, then yawned and turned onto her side, her knees drawn up and encircled by one arm. Her cheek sank into the softness of the pillow she had brought from home, the satin case smooth against her skin. The night was deep and silent, with no sound of traffic from the street. The touch came again, on her back, fingers exploring softly and carefully as though to avoid waking her, coming in contact with her skin between pajama top and the elastic at her waist.

She sucked her breath in softly. Her eyes stared blindly into the dark. Her body tensed. Horror followed the shock, rising as the fingers moved beneath the elastic waist of her pajamas and toward her buttocks. She closed her eyes tightly then, squeezing them shut against this invasion. *Oh go away, go away. Please.* How could she handle this? To face Felicia with it would be humiliating beyond anything she had ever known. It was easier to pretend she was asleep, and pray that the hand would go away, back to its own bed, and leave her alone.

As though they dared go no farther, the fingers abruptly drew away, so swiftly, so silently, that not even her bedclothes were disturbed. She continued to hold her breath, to listen, but the room was silent. There was no sound from Felicia's side of the room. After a moment Sherrie slipped out of bed and padded quickly to the bathroom and turned on the light. She stood by the doorway, her breath in halted gasps, and as her eyes adjusted in the light she peered toward

Felicia's bed. She saw the shining hair spread over the pillow. She saw the blanket drawn up over the curve of legs, hips, shoulders. There was no movement at all. Sherrie closed the door and locked it and stood there against it for several long minutes until her breathing was normal again, until she did not feel so horrified.

When she left the bathroom she went to Felicia's bed and looked down, but her room-mate seemed to be sleeping soundly, her breathing slow and deep and very quiet. Sherrie took a deep breath of her own and returned to the bathroom, put out the light, and crawled into her own bed. But this time she turned her back to the wall, and her sleep was light and restless.

She woke at the first sound of the seven o'clock bell, and was sitting on the side of her bed when Felicia finally responded to the buzzer and stretched her arms over her head. At the first sign of Felicia's awakening, Sherrie gathered her clothing quickly, ran into the bathroom and closed and locked the door. She knew as she dressed that she would never be able to be natural with Felicia again, that she did not want to room with her anymore. She had heard of girls like that, and was shocked again to know Felicia was one of them. She looked so aristocratic, so self-contained and sure of herself. She looked so queenly in her bearing, with her tall, straight body, her long hair, her pretty features. And she was so *nice*. Seemed so nice. But Sherrie knew better now, and knew she couldn't bear to be around her any more.

When she left the bathroom, Felicia was in front of her dresser brushing her hair. She was dressed in a white nightgown of opaque cotton, gathered at the throat and wrists, trimmed in red baby rick-rack. Her bare toes stuck out beneath. She was as beautiful as an angel, or a model, and Sherrie couldn't bear to look at her, to answer the smile on her lips, that smile that faltered in confusion as Sherrie passed by on her way to the door.

"Gosh, you're early," Felicia said. "Sherrie ...?"

Sherrie didn't answer. She closed the door to the room, leaving Felicia behind her, and drew a great breath of relief. Then she hurried down the stairs toward the office.

She had to wait a few minutes before Miss Aldrich beckoned her inside. The door to the outer office stood open, where a secretary worked on something at the filing cabinets. Sherrie glanced at the door, and with Miss Aldrich's nod of approval, closed it firmly.

Miss Aldrich sat behind her desk waiting, her hands clasped loosely on the polished surface, a picture of composure. She knew all of the girls by name. Knew family problems that affected their work in most cases. Sherrie was particularly familiar to her, having been at Miss Westchester's since she was nine years old. There had never been any trouble with Sherrie Manning, and Miss Aldrich was surprised to see her in the office. She was a superior student in all ways.

Sherrie said now, abruptly, "I want to change rooms, Miss Aldrich."

Miss Aldrich's smile waned a bit before it righted itself. The expression on Sherrie's face seemed a mixture of fear and embarrassment. The brown eyes did not meet hers in their usual direct way.

"Can you tell me why, Sherrie?"

"I'd rather not, Miss Aldrich."

"There is no other room available, Sherrie. You have the new girl with you, don't you? Felicia Stewart. I understand there are personality conflicts at times, but Felicia seems such a lovely person. Surely you can work it out?"

Sherrie spent a long moment looking at the floor. Miss Aldrich watched her, wondering. Felicia came from one of the best families in Virginia, so far as the records went. Her mother had gone to school here, which, the mother had said, was the reason she wanted to enroll Felicia. The school records from Felicia's former school showed no problems whatsoever, even though there was a gap of one semester between schools. Miss Aldrich had wondered about that, but Felicia's mother had not filled her in. Now, she leaned farther over her desk, her only concession to closeness with her students.

"You may feel free to tell me what the problem is, Sherrie. Everything will be confidential."

Sherrie looked up, her large, doll-clear eyes dulled. "I couldn't trade rooms with some other girl?"

"But you have occupied that room for five years, Sherrie. Are you sure you want to leave it?"

"Then would you let Felicia trade rooms with someone else?"

"Is Felicia agreeable with this change?"

"I don't know."

"You haven't discussed this with her?"

"No."

"I see," said Miss Aldrich, not seeing at all. "We really don't like to make changes so early in the semester, Sherrie. Felicia has been here only three weeks. Coming to a new school is not easy, and especially for her, since she has never been away from home before. Her mother wants her to stay here at least a month before she goes home for a weekend, because she feels she'll adjust to living away better if she remains in one place. I really can't move her to another room. And there is no other room I can let you take. I feel that you should see the counselor and talk over your problems with her if you can't tell me what they are. Perhaps both you and Felicia could talk with the counselor."

"Yes, Ma'am. Thank you," Sherrie said, and left the office with Miss Aldrich staring at her back.

Sherrie couldn't face talking to the counselor. All she wanted was a different roommate, a different room. If they wouldn't give her one, what could she do? Confront Felicia and tell her to stay on her side of the room? Keep her hands to herself? To have to admit to Felicia that she knew what kind of person she was? Oh no. Maybe it wouldn't happen again, and she could go back to being happy.

Yes, maybe.

# CHAPTER 9

Felicia noticed the change in Sherrie's attitude, the way she deliberately avoided coming near, even in the classrooms. In algebra class they had formerly sat in neighboring seats, but today Sherrie waited until Felicia was seated and then sat in the farthest away. When Felicia sought to draw her attention across the room, Sherrie ignored her. At lunch it was even worse. Sherrie went to sit at another table, drawing her friends with her, leaving Felicia to sit alone. Before the day ended, Felicia knew she was being blackballed and Sherrie's friends, all those girls who had taken Felicia into their group, were drawing away also, leaving Felicia to walk alone, sit alone, eat alone.

She was alone in the room, ready for sleep, sitting against her pillow and reading by the light of her table lamp, when Sherrie finally came in. Felicia watched her go silently to her closet, get her robe and pajamas, and lock herself in the bathroom. There were the noises then of shower, of blow-dryer, of teeth being brushed. Felicia stared at the blurring print of her book and gathered courage to talk to Sherrie. When the bathroom door opened she spoke.

"Sherrie, have I done something to upset you, to hurt your feelings or something? Very suddenly you aren't friendly any more, and I don't know why. Yesterday we were friends. Today we seem to be strangers, or worse."

Sherrie turned on her with body tensed and bent slightly forward, eyes bright with angry tears. "Oh just bug off, Felicia, just leave me alone! You're weird, you know that? You're really weird!"

Felicia dropped her book on the floor by the bed, snapped off her light and turned her face to the wall. She didn't want Sherrie to see her own tears, the display of vulnerable feelings. She had never been so insulted, so totally and rudely rejected, and her innate pride precluded any emotional display. Never would she beg for friendship. She would pretend she did not care in the least. She heard Sherrie flop into her own bed and the room went dark. There was nothing more to say. Not even the usual goodnight.

Felicia cried herself to sleep, softly, sobs smothered in her pillow, huddling with body curled as near the wall as she could get, wishing she were home in her own bed, wishing she were in baby Jeremy's nursery, sitting in the rocking chair by the windows, with him cuddled warm and accepting in her arms. Tonight she needed him even more than he needed her. He was all right without her. Mama said so, every week when they talked on the phone: "He's doing very well, Felicia. He doesn't miss you at all. Don't worry about him. He and Louise are getting along fine. Thank God." Felicia was glad Jeremy liked Louise, but tonight her arms ached to hold him, to have him need and want her again. She even missed and longed for the ghostly touch of his hands in the dark of night, that calling that no longer reached her. She drifted to sleep with his image in her mind, the memory of his softness in her arms.

Sherrie couldn't escape. It was a nightmare in which she couldn't move. The hands came in beneath her bedclothes and began stroking her softly, stealthily, all over from her neck down, cold fingers going from gentle to urgent to brutal, as though trying to wake her, nails biting into soft flesh of breast and buttock and inner thigh. They came out of the dark, curved and clawed and evil, and she was cornered in her bed and unable to escape. The hands touched her, and the touch was of hatred. And at last she woke, suddenly, violently, as the hands gripped her body and pulled her toward the side of the bed. She screamed once, a long, quivering cry of terror as she wrenched away and rolled over the foot of her bed, tumbling in the dark to the floor, scrambling up and feeling with desperate hands along the wall for the bathroom door and safety, sobs in her throat, fear dragging her down and keeping her in nightmare slowness.

The room was light suddenly, and she whirled to see Felicia staring from her bed, her hand still resting on the lamp at her bedside. It was that lamp that had removed the darkness, turned on by Felicia's own hand. It seemed somehow to add to the horror of what Felicia had done to her, as though she wanted to see Sherrie's reaction, to see her face twisted by terror, her hands groping like a trapped and blinded animal.

"Sherrie!" Felicia cried, pulling her legs from the bed, her night-gown twisting up to her hips as she moved and stood up, the night-gown falling again to touch her bare feet. Sherrie stared, unable to move, and watched Felicia take several steps toward her. "What's wrong?" Felicia was asking, her face revealing a kind of horror of her own.

Sherrie pushed against the wall. "Get away from me! Please! Don't touch me!"

Felicia stopped, staring. Her hands raised and dropped, once. "Did you have a bad dream, Sherrie?"

"Oh, God!" Sherrie took a few hesitant steps toward the door to the hall; then, passing as far as the room allowed from Felicia, she began running, stumbling, sobbing as she ran. When she reached the door she wrenched it open with both hands and flung it back against the wall. She ran down the hall, her voice unnatural and choked with half-screams, half-sobs. Doors along the hall opened and faces looked out, but Sherrie didn't see them. She found the stairs and stumbled down.

Felicia stood in the middle of the room, unmoving, stunned. A couple of the girls in drooping, wrinkled pajamas passed the open door, glanced in, and went on. Footsteps rang on the uncarpeted floor as someone hurried. Felicia saw Miss Aldrich go by.

Sherrie was huddled in a chair in the office when Miss Aldrich found her.

Felicia sat on her bed, waiting. Time moved slowly on toward dawn, and the house was quiet again, the footsteps in the hall gone now. She chewed on her thumbnail relentlessly, peeling it off thin strip by strip. Her hands shook. Dread tightened her scalp. Sherrie had not returned. Felicia was afraid, but did not know why. Something terrible had happened, was happening, and she felt responsible.

At seven o'clock, just after the ring of the morning buzzer, a young, solemn face peered in at her.

"Are you Felicia Stewart?"

"Yes."

"Miss Aldrich wants to see you in the office as soon as you can get dressed."

She withdrew as suddenly as she had appeared, without waiting for a reply. Felicia dressed hurriedly, nervously, instinctively choosing a modest blouse and skirt. The high round collar covered her throat. The pleats of the skirt hung loosely over her hips. The crepe rubber soles of her shoes squished quietly on the wood floors as she went out and down the stairs.

Miss Aldrich sat behind her desk with her hands folded, waiting. But there were two other people in the room also. One of them was a middle-aged woman whom Felicia had not seen before, and the other was Sherrie, sitting turned away in her chair, her chin resting on her fist, her eyes carefully avoiding Felicia. She was still dressed in pajamas, but someone had draped a shawl over her shoulders.

Miss Aldrich said, "Felicia, this is Mrs. Hall, one of our counselors. Sit down, please. We need to hear your explanation about last night."

Felicia looked at the faces in the room, at the composed masks of the two older women, of the still rejection of Sherrie's.

"I — I was awakened by Sherrie screaming, crying, having a bad nightmare. I turned on the light. She ran out of the room. That's all I know." What did they want her to tell them? They were waiting, expecting more. But she didn't know what they wanted to hear.

Miss Aldrich finally said, "This is a delicate and embarrassing matter, for all of us. If you can give any reasonable explanation, we might be able to keep you here at school. We certainly don't want any kind of publicity about this. But we hesitate even to put into the room of another girl someone who behaves as Sherrie says you behaved. Mrs. Hall felt, if you would accept counseling, that perhaps — "

Felicia interrupted quietly, her voice in soft contrast to the sudden rage within her. "What have I been accused of?"

All three pairs of eyes looked at her, and Sherrie's gleamed with hatred. "As if you didn't know!" she cried. "There she sits acting like — "

"Sherrie!" Miss Aldrich said sharply. "That will get us nowhere. I understand how you feel, but —

Again Felicia interrupted. "I *said*, what have I been accused of?"

Mrs. Hall said in a gentle and impartial voice, "You have been accused of lesbianism. Of coming to Sherrie's bed in the night and putting your hands on her."

Sherrie sat up in her chair and cried shrilly, "It was more than that! She was trying to frighten me, to get even with me for snubbing her. *She tried to drag me out of my bed.*" Sherrie began to weep, covering her face with her hands. Miss Aldrich got up immediately and went to her, laying a hand on the bowed shoulders.

Felicia's mind found the truth swiftly. Her hands went to her mouth, folded one over the other, to stop the blurting of an explanation they would neither understand nor accept. Her eyes stared at the people in the room, scarcely seeing.

They saw her widened eyes over the tops of her hands, and found even that difficult to understand.

Mrs. Hall said, "Do you have anything to say, Felicia?"

Felicia dropped her hands to her lap. They were cold as death now. "No, Ma'am, except, I didn't do anything." She stared at the wall ahead of her. *Hands in the night, tiny, cold, capable of gentle caresses or cruel pinches and tugs. Was it gathering strength, this thing which reached out from her baby? Had he been searching for her, and found instead someone who would never understand*?

"Felicia," Mrs. Hall said, "Sherrie has been here at Miss Westchester's for five years. She does not have a record of lying nor of hysteria. She has never had any trouble with a roommate before. On the other hand, you have been here a little over three weeks. We do not know you very well. If Sherrie comes to us, crying in the night, and tells us you have been touching her, and trying to frighten her, what are we to think?"

Felicia said, "Was she hurt?"

"Not physically."

"Couldn't it just have been a bad dream she was having?" Felicia asked hopefully, praying in her heart that Sherrie might be persuaded to agree, that it be so, yet knowing instinctively Sherrie had not dreamed it. He had been there, at last, in his strange, disembodied way.

*But why had he gone to Sherrie*?

Mrs. Hall said, "Sherrie does not feel it was a dream, Felicia."

Miss Aldrich came back to her chair, glanced at a file that lay open on her desk. "Go on to your classes, Felicia. I must ask your mother to come in and have a talk about this."

"Oh, please don't do that," Felicia cried softly, "don't tell her what Sherrie said, please!"

"We have to discuss this with your mother, Felicia. She does have a right to know. She's your legal guardian, she enrolled you here, and since we may be forced to expel you, she has to know."

Felicia was shaking her head. "No, please. Isn't there anything I can do to make up to Sherrie for — for what happened? I'm sorry, I really am. Couldn't you just let me have a room alone?" *And yet, if Mama knows, she might take me home again, and I'll be with Jeremy for the rest of our lives* ... But she would never understand. Never. When she had thought there was sex with boys she had been repelled, hurt, disbelieving. She would never tolerate this thing. And telling her the truth was impossible. Impossible to explain, impossible to understand, to accept.

"Go to your classes, Felicia," Miss Aldrich said icily. "And then be packed and ready to go when your mother comes. I feel sure we won't be able to keep you here at school."

"Aren't you even going to give me a second chance?"

"In a sense you've had a second chance. Sherrie requested a change in roommates yesterday."

Felicia left the room with no further argument. She went upstairs and collected her books for class, even though she knew she would not be able to concentrate.

THE BABY SMILED at Louise for the first time, that morning, a sudden, wide, round, toothless smile of delight, and bowed his body upwards from the cradle eager to be lifted. Louise responded with even more delight, feeling wanted for the first time since she had started taking care of him. He had been a puzzle to her, making her feel about as human as a robot. He had merely tolerated the baths, the changes, the feeding; and her original nervousness and awkwardness had stayed with her. She had been amazed last week when Mrs. Stewart told her she had cancelled the offer to the new nurse, and gave the position to Louise permanently.

Louise was only half pleased. She had discussed it with her fiancé, Rob, and together they decided the extra thousand dollars a month would go a long way in furnishing their home, and, for that matter, in making sure there would be a home. Unlike Louise, Rob had grown up with little brothers and sisters and was able to reassure her. "How old is he? Between three and four months? Well, they don't do much at that age anyway, even if they're healthy and normal, and if he never cries he may be a deaf mute, and he may be a little retarded or something. I wouldn't worry about it. If she thinks you're doing a great job, you can be sure you're doing a great job. And anyway, you need the experience, for I've got plans for you." And as usual their conversation was lost somewhere. She had only one night off a week now.

Still feeling awkward, and a bit afraid that she might drop him, Louise slipped her hands under Jeremy's back and lifted him out of the cradle. His toothless gums were pink in the wide open grin. His tongue nudged them playfully. Louise returned the smile, but she said nothing. She had never been able to bring herself to talk to him. It seemed somehow senseless and useless and unwanted. There had been so many times when she felt uncomfortable in his presence. In his solemn staring at the ceiling he had seemed to be thinking old thoughts, solving problems, figuring solutions, so that she felt obliged to tiptoe about the room and keep as quiet as possible. Her fiancé had told her that was ridiculous, and she believed him, but it hadn't help her to change her feelings. For the first time now she felt Jeremy's babyhood, and it gave her a warm delight she had not experienced before.

Mildred came into the nursery just as Louise drew the baby to her breast. Louise only glanced at her. But here was someone to whom she could express her feelings.

"He smiled at me, Mrs. Stewart! Did you see that? Look at him, he's almost laughing."

Mildred came near and looked down and with one finger nudged his round cheek. "Good morning, Jeremy. How nice to see you smiling. What a nice nursey you have, ummm?"

The phone began ringing in Mildred's private sitting room, a distant and beckoning sound. It drew the attention of all three, baby Jeremy as much as the others. He seemed to be listening intently, his smile gone, his mouth only slightly open now. Louise, looking at him, remembered Rob saying he might be a deaf mute, and knew that at least he was not deaf. He had heard the phone ringing as clearly as she had, as Mildred Stewart had.

Mildred said, frowning faintly, "Who on earth could be calling at this time of day?" Not waiting for an answer, Mildred swept out toward her suite.

Louise looked down at Jeremy again, and saw that his head was turned toward the door, that he was still listening intently. Only when the phone stopped ringing did his body relax, the tension cease, and the smile return. He put both fists in his mouth and grinned behind them up at Louise, his eyes sparkling with a kind of mischief that made Louise laugh.

In her sitting room, Mildred sat at her desk, leaning an elbow on the leather pad, cradling the phone between her shoulder and her left ear. The moment she had heard Miss Aldrich's voice she knew something was wrong. Very seriously wrong.

"Is Felicia ill?" Mildred asked immediately.

"No, Mrs. Stewart, Felicia is not at all ill. She's been doing very well in her school work, and seemed to be doing well socially and as far as the usual homesickness goes. This is a different situation, Mrs. Stewart, and something I can't talk about on the phone. I would rather you came up as soon as possible. I'm afraid you'll have to be prepared to take Felicia home with you."

"Why on earth? You said she was doing well in school, and is not ill. Is it an unexpected closing of the school?"

"No, nothing like that. I'm afraid, Mrs. Stewart, that Miss Westchester's can't have Felicia as a student any more. I'm very sorry to say we're expelling her."

"*Expelling her*!" Mildred stood, shoving her chair backwards. "If she's a good student, if she's — What has she done to deserve — ?" Expelled. A word of disgrace. Only the least desirable, the incorrigible or depraved were expelled. At least in her day. And now, her own daughter, her Felicia?

"Mrs. Stewart!" Miss Aldrich was demanding, almost shouting. "Please. You must come up to school so we can discuss this with you."

Mildred groped behind her blindly, pulled the chair forward, and sank into it. When she spoke again her voice was calm and cold. "Yes, I'll come immediately, Miss Aldrich. I'll be there in a few hours." *And,* she added to herself, *you had better make this good, lady, or I'll sue the roof right off your supercilious head.*

Before she started dressing, she called the garage and told Clint to bring the limousine around for a trip to Washington. She heard the lift of pleasure in his voice when he answered. The days of chauffeuring were slipping farther and farther into the past for Clint, now that Grandmother Marchant was dead, and now also that gas prices made the use of the limousine look ridiculous and selfish — downright hoggish. But Mildred did not feel up to driving the trip to the school, and did not want to fly. She wanted to be able to stare out the window and try to figure this thing out, and she knew Clint would drive in silence in his well-mannered way.

Mildred finished dressing — black suit, white blouse and scarf, white gloves — and at the last moment added an accessory she seldom wore: a small hat with veil that would help conceal her eyes and face.

When she went downstairs Clint was waiting for her, the limousine glistening blackly from fresh polishing and the September sun. Mildred paused only to tell Celta where she was going and when she expected to return. Celta, accustomed to questioning Mildred as she would her own daughter, saw Mildred's face and decided to wait until later to find out the reason for the trip. She knew, of course, that it had something to do with Felicia, and she hoped that Mildred would be bringing the girl home, for Celta had missed her dearly.

# CHAPTER 10

Louise, filled with her unexpected success with the baby that morning, was learning how to play baby games. All afternoon she had been making funny faces, and various formless sounds, pleased by his delighted smiles. She wanted now to hear him laugh, and she held him above her face and brought him down slowly and pretended to bite his belly. He kicked his legs and waved his arms, rocking in her hands, and grinned all the wider, but the out-loud laughter was missing. Louise raised him into the air again, her head tipped back, and watched the pink toothless gums, the fascinated round smile. His hands reached for her face, and she began bringing him down slowly toward her.

"I'm gonna bite you now — eat baby all up — gonna bite that baby's tummy." Slowly, so slowly downward, while his hands reached and his smile became a silent O of anticipation ... slowly, so slowly, and then a pretend mouthful of baby's tummy ...

She screamed. A startled rush of agony, of protest as his fingers clawed her face, as his thumbs dug into her eyes as though to dislodge the eyeballs, to rake them out and leave them hanging on her blood-stained cheeks. She dropped him, yet he clung to her, hooking his thumbs and fingers. She stumbled blindly across the nursery and fell to her knees, her hands trembling, shaking, clawing at those tiny hands that tortured her.

She freed herself as her screams echoed back at her from somewhere in the depths of the house, and crawled to her feet and ran for the door, bumping into the wall, turning, reaching, screaming, screaming, feeling hot blood on her cheeks.

HANDS GRIPPED her shoulders suddenly and Celta cried, "My Lord, Louise! What happened? Hush! Hush it up now!"

Celta's cool, strong hands guided her through the doorway, around a corner, through another doorway which Louise's shoulder scraped, and bent her forward over something.

"Here, here," Celta ordered, her voice harsh with anxiety, "Get your hands down and let me wash your face. Here, sit down on the toilet and stop your screaming and your shaking. It's all right, it's all right."

She sat with her head tipped back, the pain in her eyes worse than any she had ever felt, and Celta bathed her face in cool water. Sobs jerked her body. Fear made her tremble.

"My eyes! Oh, my eyes, Celta. I'm blind."

"No, no you're not. Try opening them now."

As she tried, the pain increased, and she stopped. But she had seen the merest slit of light, of blurred blue-and-white checked apron; she recalled seeing Celta wearing it earlier.

"What on earth happened, Louise?" Celta asked. "You look like you met up with a wildcat right out of the woods. Scratches all around your eyes. I'll get someone to take you to a doctor if it looks like you need one, once I get you cleaned up a bit. Come on. I'll lead you downstairs."

Louise clung to her, walking slowly, afraid to try to open her eyes. "He did it," she said faintly. And then she remembered, and stopped walking, and found she could open her eyes after all, that they burned no worse when open than closed. The pain seemed now to be lessening, and with it the intense, helpless fear. Mrs. Stewart had left the baby in her care, and she had dropped him on the floor. "Celta, I dropped the baby. I don't know where. I can't just leave him there, but Celta, I can't go back in there. I can't."

Celta hesitated only a moment. She patted Louise's shoulder with sympathy. "I'll go. Let's get you downstairs first," she said.

MISS WESTCHESTER'S was quiet when Mildred stepped out of the limousine and walked up the steps and into the long hall. The late afternoon classes were in progress, and from various rooms along the hall she could hear the voices of an occasional teacher or student. There was a faint school-roomish smell of books, chalk, erasers and floor polish. But today it was a stifling smell. Almost nauseating. That it had once seemed pleasant was forgotten. She entered the office and was shown immediately in to see Miss Aldrich. The door closed behind her, and the low-volume sounds of the classrooms were eliminated. There were only Miss Aldrich's footsteps going back to her desk, and the whisper of the leather chair as Mildred sat down. She waited, her lips tightly compressed. She was not going to make this any easier on Miss Aldrich than was necessary.

Miss Aldrich couldn't seem to meet Mildred Stewart's cold and steady gaze. She had been dreading this meeting all day. She had tried to think of ways to say what she must say, but none of them seemed adequate. She had decided on a direct approach.

"Mrs. Stewart, a complaint against Felicia has been lodged by her roommate, Sherrie. More than once. The first time Sherrie, and the problem, was ignored, I'm sorry to say, for the second time she was terrified and refused to go back into the room with Felicia. It seems that during the night Felicia came to Sherrie's bed and made ... sexual overtures. There simply is no other explanation for what she was doing. And of course there's no other solution but for you to remove Felicia from our school. I'm sorry. We simply cannot have her here at Miss Westchester's."

Mildred's control had slackened gradually, collapsing at last, dragging her face down, making her look twenty years beyond her age. She whispered loudly, "*Lesbianism?*" Of all things that had entered her mind on the drive up to Washington, that had not been one of them.

She had visualized boys crawling in and out of windows in the night. She had imagined her daughter changed from a serious, angel-faced girl into a wanton, climbing out her window and down the wall to a night on the town; she had seen her telling everyone about her past, about the baby, and making herself a reputation the school could not allow. But not once had she thought of sex with another girl.

"I'm afraid so, Mrs. Stewart," Miss Aldrich said.

"I don't believe this. I demand to see this girl, this roommate, and to hear this accusation myself! I want to see my daughter."

But there was sex with a boy once, maybe more than once, and she hadn't believed that at first either. If Felicia would have sex with a boy at age thirteen ... then why did she doubt ...?

She wished suddenly that she could walk out and never see anyone at all. Not the roommate. Not Felicia.

But Miss Aldrich was already out of the office, and there was nothing for Mildred to do but wait, and rise and pace the floor like a caged animal.

The time passed in exaggerated slowness. Mildred wished she had demanded that Miss Aldrich tell her this problem over the phone. She wished ... God, she wished that she had never had a child at all!

A whisper of sound, and Mildred whirled to see Miss Aldrich lead the girls into the room. The smaller girl glanced only briefly at Mildred before she lowered her eyes. Mildred glanced at her just as briefly. Then she met Felicia's eyes. Felicia looked at her with large, hurting eyes; eyes filled with regret and guilt. Mildred knew her daughter's expressions, and the look in those eyes gave her a sorrow such as she had never known before. She wanted both to take the girl into her arms and protect her forever, and to push her away, never see her again as long as she lived.

Mildred turned away and pressed her fingers to her lips for a moment, swallowing the knot of emotion the best she could. She could not burst into tears, not here, not in front of them. It was not the Marchant way.

"Felicia, is what they say about you true?"

"Mama ..." Felicia said softly.

"Don't make excuses, please. Just tell the truth."

"I did not do what she said I did, Mama. I didn't go to her bed. *I wouldn't do that."*

"Then why are they doing this to us?"

But the other girl half-cried, half-screamed, "She's lying! She was there! I felt her hands! She was feeling me all over, and then she tried to pull me out of the bed! Of course she's lying to you! Can't you see that?"

Miss Aldrich touched Sherrie on the shoulder and cautioned her to silence.

Mildred turned and faced Felicia, and saw tears now, and more fear and guilt. "Felicia, why would she say these things?" And in the fear and guilt on Felicia's face she read what she felt was the truth, and she remembered that sexual acts had led to the pregnancy, and knew Sherrie was not the one who was lying. She turned her back again, and went to look out the window. Behind her Sherrie tried to muffle sobs.

Miss Aldrich said, "There's no reason to continue this, is there, Mrs. Stewart?"

"You're right, Miss Aldrich," Mildred said. "Take them both away, please. I need to talk with you."

There were soft footsteps on the hardwood floors, crepe soles squishing, and the closing of the door. Miss Aldrich's footsteps came back to the desk. Mildred let her wait while she gathered her courage to face her, to do what she had to do. At last she turned and sat in front of the desk, facing Miss Aldrich. She was thankful for the veil and the small privacy it gave her.

"Miss Aldrich, I can't handle this. I seem to have given my daughter none of my own values. I don't understand it at all. I thought I knew her. Even after last year I thought I knew her. But I don't." Miss Aldrich did not ask about last year, but was pleased to note that her suspicions of previous problems had been correct.

Mildred opened her handbag and took a small engraved card from her wallet. She placed it on the desk. "That is the name and telephone number of Felicia's father. His address is there, too. It's near Los Angeles. Call him, and tell him to expect Felicia. Then put her on the first plane to Los Angeles. Tell him she is his responsibility now. Maybe he is the one she has needed all this time."

Miss Aldrich stared at her, astonishment written on every feature of her face, her fingers automatically picking up and rubbing the card. Mildred stood and went toward the door without looking back. There she paused only a moment, her head down.

"Tell him ... tell him she needs psychiatric care."

She went out of the office, out of the school, and got into the car.

"Home, Clint. Please," she said softly. Looking out of the window, she tried to think of nothing.

LEAVING LOUISE DOWNSTAIRS, Celta returned to the nursery. The baby was on the floor by the cradle. He had turned over onto his stomach and was crawling, with one plump knee drawn up to push himself along, his hands reaching for support, just inches away from the base of his cradle. He tipped his head back and looked steadily into Celta's eyes, pausing in his slow progress. It was the first time Celta had seen him in weeks, and then she had been at a distance, out in the garden with Felicia. She saw now a beautiful baby with large dark blue eyes, long lashes, thin little wing brows, a perfectly formed mouth whose lower lip hung down moistly. He watched Celta with curiosity and innocence. He could have been any normal five-month-old baby, but Celta knew he wasn't. She bent down to pick him up and put him back into his cradle, and saw stains of blood under his sharp little fingernails.

She hesitated, but only for a moment. Mildred would be coming home soon, and perhaps bringing Felicia with her, and of all things Felicia must not see the baby as she was seeing him. Poor Felicia; Celta had seen the helpless love of child-mother for infant son. As for Mildred, she had tried to tell her the truth right back in the beginning, before Felicia had gotten so attached to him, back when he should have been taken away and kept away, but Mildred didn't want to know. And now Celta saw that it was too late. Only the devil himself knew the dark powers in this changeling, and putting him away now might do more harm than good. It was up to her now. She must watch this one, see after him herself.

Celta lifted Jeremy cautiously, old eyes meeting young, mind attempting to read mind and perhaps, in one case, succeeding. The baby lay limp in her hands, arms and legs hanging, but she held him at arm's length, knowing he could change with the blink of an eye. Instead of putting him into the small cradle, she put him into the large crib, and raised and locked the side. His eyes left hers and flicked quickly around the crib, observing the stout vertical bars.

"You're not going to get out of there, my lad, for quite some time yet," Celta said calmly. "And you might as well behave yourself, for you're not going to dragoon this old lady, not if I can help it, and I aim to try, you'll see. And you might as well keep your little claws to yourself, because someone's got to feed you yet, and give you your bath now and then, because you're not up to walking and taking care of yourself. You had better behave yourself. Do you understand what I'm saying?"

She brought a wet washcloth from the bathroom and washed the drying blood from the end of each little finger. He stared into her face, his hands limp in hers, unresisting. But she did lot lower her guard against him. She held his hands firmly, the pressure of her fingers making red marks in the soft flesh of his arms.

When his fingernails were pink and white again she took the washcloth back into the bathroom and rinsed it out carefully before dropping it into the hamper.

Then she went downstairs to Louise. Louise could see her way now, through blurred pain and soreness, but her confidence was almost totally destroyed.

"I thought he liked me after all," she said, half in tears, her voice a soft whine. "This morning he really wanted me to pick him up, and all day he has acted like he really liked me. It was like he all of a sudden got real happy, you know? And then his face got that funny look like he usually has only which I didn't know about until I saw him change from happy to kind of glum again, you know what I mean? And he reached his hands into my face ... and ... it might not have hurt so much if his fingers weren't so small ... I don't know, don't understand it at all. It was like all of sudden he absolutely hated me."

"Ummhuh," Celta commented through close lips.

"Now I've lost my job, Celta, all of it, because I can't go back up there, ever, and Mrs. Stewart would never understand. If I tried to tell her what happened she would probably think I was exaggerating, just like she did all those other nurses that quit. And you know that's true. I hear her sometimes. Babies don't deliberately do mean things like that, she'll say; I heard her when I was passing by the office a couple of times when nurses would quit. Babies don't spit all over a person on purpose, like they said he did, and they don't pull hair out in a handful on purpose like they said he did. They were being ridiculous, she said, and you know what, Celta? I thought she was right. I thought to myself, that's stupid for nurses to claim that! I've never been around babies much, but any fool would know they're innocent as the driven dawn, just like baby kittens or puppies or my little thing. They haven't learned to be mean yet. Nobody has taught them how. But now I've changed my mind, because I swear to you, Celta, that baby upstairs was *trying to kill me*!"

"Ummmhuh." Celta showed none of the surprise that Louise expected, nor even a change of expression on her set, wrinkled face. She continued leading Louise toward the back of the house, where they would probably find someone to drive her to town.

"And Celta," Louise said, "I can't tell Mrs. Stewart that because she'd swear I was insane. So what do I do?"

"Why don't I just find someone to drive you to a doctor first, Louise — "

"No. I can drive myself. I'd rather. I can see well enough now and I'd like to take the rest of the day off."

"If I were you, Louise, I'd just look for another job."

"You would?" Surprised relief was in Louise's voice. That was what she wanted to hear, but had not expected. "If I quit without notice, would Mrs. Stewart give me good recommendations?"

"I'll see that she does, Louise. Don't worry about it. Just go on home, plan your wedding, and be happy."

"I don't think I ever want to have a baby."

"*Nonsense.*" Celta said sharply. "You go ahead and have a houseful of babies, and enjoy them. They'll be just as sweet and adorable as you were when you were a baby. This one ... the one upstairs ... is not normal, Louise."

Louise peered at Celta. "Not normal? What do you mean?"

Celta stared straight ahead, past the umbrella stand at the end of the downstairs hall, through the glass door to the terrace at the back of the house, into the dark rise of the forested hill. She hadn't meant to say so much. But now that she had, she couldn't let it hang. "Just not normal, Louise. Hadn't you noticed he never utters a sound? There's something not right. But don't you go and talk about it to anyone at all, you hear. Just forget it." She added, on the verge of blackmail, "I'll see to it that you get the best recommendations."

*If*, her silence implied, you say nothing at all. She stood at the door and watched Louise leave. The young woman went toward the garage, out of sight around the shrubs at the edge of the terrace, her sweater and purse from the hall closet in her hands. A moment later Celta heard the cough of her little car.

Celta went slowly back upstairs, looked in on Jeremy from the doorway and saw him sitting up in his crib, looking through the bars at her. He had no toys whatsoever with him. Would he notice a toy if it were given to him? She felt a touch of sadness as she looked at him, a faint stirring of pity. He looked so much like Felicia at five months, except he was a larger, huskier baby than she had been. Also, he was sitting up, had pulled himself into that position without help. Celta wondered how long it would be before he found a way to climb out of his crib ... his prison, she admitted to herself.

And what would happen then?

She went in, over to the overloaded toy box in the corner of the room. She chose toys that had been Felicia's, that her dear child had given to Jeremy; a threadbare little brown bear with one bead eye missing, its ears chewed and drooping. She chose an often-washed stuffed dog, little and soft and squeezable. She chose a new rubber ball, and a larger plastic ball whose interior was filled with marbles or something that rattled. She dropped them all into the crib.

Jeremy had watched her, sitting limp and still, his hands folded together between his bent knees. His eyes bored into hers, not wavering, nor blinking, nor moving at any time toward the toys that rolled against his legs.

Celta felt that he was trying to read her mind, that he was reaching into her, invading her every thought and feeling. Tears filled her eyes suddenly as she stood back, well away from him.

"Why couldn't you just be a good baby, Jeremy?" she asked softly, whispering in the still room. "Why couldn't you be? Like your mother was?"

The lights were on in the house when Mildred came home and climbed the stairs to her rooms. She was unpleasantly surprised to find Celta sitting in a straight chair by the hall door to the nursery. Mildred had wanted to go straight to bed. The lights of the nursery, brighter than those of the hallway, threw a long, crooked shadow across the carpet. Celta stood up.

"Where's Louise?" Mildred asked, just as Celta asked, "Where's Felicia?" And then for a long moment they simply stared at each other.

Mildred looked past Celta and saw Jeremy sitting in the corner of the crib. He looked tiny and lost and so much like Felicia that Mildred almost lost control. To weep in front of Celta would not be as humiliating as to weep in front of anyone else. Still, she was determined to wait until she was locked in her own room.

Celta said, "Louise took sick and had to leave. She won't be coming back."

"Oh Lord. I have to start looking for yet another nurse."

"No. I'll take care of him myself from now on. You can do without me downstairs now; the new maid seems to be settling in all right."

Mildred drew a long breath. Jeremy hadn't moved. He sat in his corner staring at her, and even though she couldn't see his eyes clearly it seemed he was glaring, brows lowered into a faint frown, small mouth drooping. Perhaps it was the light that made him seem so fierce, so filled with hate. Of course it had to be the light.

"Felicia isn't coming home," she said then.

If Celta answered, Mildred didn't notice. Jeremy had moved suddenly. He leaned forward, going down on hands and knees, and hurried to the nearest side of the crib, where his hands gripped two vertical bars tightly. He pulled himself up and pushed his face between the bars, and in the shadow of the crib his features seemed twisted with reptilian rage.

But of course it was only the strange fall of the light across his face, and her own emotional exhaustion. She went on to her room, cutting off Celta's questions about Felicia. She couldn't face them; not tonight.

Not until later did Mildred wonder at Jeremy's sudden mobility. Wasn't he crawling and pulling up earlier than most babies? He wasn't quite five months old. He wouldn't be five months old until the twelfth of October, another week away.

She refused to think about him. Felicia ...

# CHAPTER 11

Felicia's father met her with reluctance. She could see it in his awkward smile, his glances that avoided direct contact with her eyes.

Leonard Stewart was deeply uncomfortable. His two-bedroom apartment was not meant for sharing with a teenage daughter. He didn't have the wealth of the Marchant family, and when he divorced Mildred Marchant he had traded money for freedom. Of course he would take in his daughter, and keep her until he could decide what to do with her, but he never had known her very well, he realized, and she was a stranger now. He had felt that she was somehow too boy-crazy, too sexy with boys. After all, she had already had a baby. And only fourteen now, and the baby how old? Four or five months. And then to hear from whatshername that his daughter was being expelled from the girls' school because of sexual activities! He could only draw the conclusion that she was some kind of degenerate, a nymphomaniac of both persuasions. Whatever she was, he had no intentions of discussing it with her. He could talk about sex with other men, with the women he slept with, but in no way was he going to talk about sex with his daughter. He felt swift, sharp anger at his wife. His ex-wife now. What was the matter with her that she was disowning, practically disowning, her own daughter just because of this thing? What kind of mother was she?

"Did you have a nice trip?" he asked, eyes on the road.

"Okay. It was okay," she said dully. He sensed her unhappiness, but that too embarrassed him.

Felicia felt tired, but her thoughts were wide awake, no more inclined to give her rest now than they had on the plane coming west, nor during the long hours after she had learned her mother no longer wanted her at all, that she didn't even care enough to say goodbye. Felicia was numb, the hurting so far buried inside her that it was simply her inner self, never to be escaped. And her father's attitude, so obvious — as though he wanted to run away from her, as though to get lost in the crowd of the airport terminal would be the best thing that could happen to him. But she was compliant yet. A fourteen year old whose fifteenth birthday was still almost six weeks away, who had been accustomed all her life to obeying, to being cared for. Her dad didn't want her either, but he at least had met her and was taking her home with him.

UNTIL HE SAW her at the airport, Leonard Stewart had thought of Felicia — when he thought of her — as still a little girl. Now he noticed that she was slim and lovely with definite curves. Her hair and face were beautiful, even with the still sadness and longing in her eyes; or perhaps because of those qualities. He had nothing to say to her.

She had nothing to say to him, either. The only remark she made when he showed her the small apartment, and her own small room, was: "Do you mind if I keep a night light on?"

He looked at her sharply. Afraid of the dark? He shrugged. "Sure, leave it on." He glanced at his watch. "Look, Felicia, I have to get back to the office ..."

She nodded, and he escaped. He had shown her where the television was, and the stereo; and the refrigerator, cold and white in the kitchen. He had pointed out the park, and its facilities, including the swimming pool, all within walking distance. On the way from the airport, he had also shown her where the school was and informed her she'd be enrolling there on Monday.

Felicia began to unpack. It was the tenth of October.

It was the tenth of October. For the last two weeks of October, Mildred hardly left her room. She could forget about the baby now, for Celta had indeed set herself up as Jeremy's nurse, his constant companion, and it was a great load off Mildred's mind. But she couldn't forget the other thing ... the complete loss of her daughter, that sickening thing her daughter had done, the feeling of failure on her own part. For she did feel responsible. And that she could not accept. It was Felicia's own doing, not hers. It must have been a strain of evil in the Stewart family. No Marchant had ever done these horrible things. Again the thought would come: It was her fault. She was Felicia's mother, after all. She must have failed. But where?

She felt less and less able to leave her bed. Time after time her hand would rest on the bedside phone, a frown of indecision on her forehead. She wanted to call Felicia, to speak to her, to tell her ... what? Time after time her hand would slip away.

Three postcards from Leonard told her that Felicia had arrived safely; that she had started school, that she was settling in.

As October melted into November, the fall colors outside her window dropped away and left the naked branches of gray winter. Felicia's birthday came; Mildred sent her a card, and a check. She was unable to make herself telephone.

Felicia didn't call her, either.

She began hearing the sounds on November 10.

At first she thought it was an animal in the woods behind the house, a very young animal, lost from its mother perhaps. The sound was one of the most melancholy she had ever heard. It was a pleading, a calling, a weeping ... it was indescribable and heartbreaking.

She left her bed, her mind drawn from her own problems, and opened the window. A cold rain was falling in the black night. As her hair dampened and her skin grew icy she listened, but there was nothing now but the gentle sound of falling rain, dripping through the trees onto dead autumn leaves. She drew back, oddly disturbed, feeling in her own heart the distress of that young one who had lost its mother.

She listened long into the night, under her warm blankets, but there was nothing more. Eventually she slept. The next day she recalled it like a vivid dream. But by the time night came again the cry had slipped into the recesses of her mind.

It awakened her. A far-away calling, somewhere beyond the walls, lonely crying, desperate crying, moving in waves like seashore tides, coming in, in, almost reaching safety, and drawing away, farther and farther.

She sat up in bed, listening. The sound was changing, becoming angry. And now it seemed to be forming vowels, almost speaking. She felt she could understand if only she could hear it more clearly. But still she didn't go to the window. She huddled instead, sitting up, drawing her blanket tight around her chest, and wished simply that the creature would stop crying and go away and leave her in peace. Angrily, she vowed to send Clint into the woods tomorrow to find that little lost creature and put it out of its misery.

Why did it cry only at night ?

She turned on her bedside lamp and saw the hour was close to three. The hour in which death came closest to the earth. The hour of silence, of lonely wakefulness. The hour when the deserted searched the darkness for shelter.

And the hour of birth.

She was suddenly aware of silence. She was not even sure at what point the animal had stopped its wailing.

After several minutes, Mildred turned out her light again and lay down. From the hall downstairs came the melodic chime of fifteen minutes past the hour, the only voice in the world at that moment, it seemed. She closed her eyes with determination.

Like mist rising from the river, the weeping began again. Suddenly she knew it for what it was, and with a sense of shock she was up and standing beside her bed. *The baby was crying.* It was not an animal in the woods, but Jeremy here in the house, his strange, untried weeping sounding alien and lost and far away. For the first time in his life Jeremy was crying.

Where was Celta? Was she sleeping so soundly that she hadn't heard him? How could anyone not hear that terrible, plaintive cry?

She didn't bother to grab her robe or slippers, but rushed down the hall to the nursery. When she wrenched the door open, soft light beckoned her in.

She stopped and stared. The room was as silent as death.

Celta stood at the side of the crib, staring down, her hands gripping the top rail. Her hair was hanging down her back, braided for the night in a thin rope of gray. An old bathrobe hung crookedly from her bony shoulders.

Mildred walked slowly into the room. Softly, so as not to start the baby crying again, she said, "I thought you hadn't heard him."

Celta whirled, and for a moment looked as though she might faint. She put one hand to her heart and closed her eyes briefly. Mildred took her arm, concerned.

"Celta?"

The elderly woman shook her head. "It's all right. I'm all right. I didn't hear you come in."

"I heard the baby crying ..." But she was looking past Celta into the crib. Jeremy was lying as still as a doll, his small arms flung wide, his palms toward the ceiling, his eyes partly opened but unseeing, his mouth open slightly. "Celta, what's wrong with him?"

"That's just one of his spells," Celta said in an undertone.

"His spells?" Mildred leaned over the side of the crib. She touched his cheek, and found it cold. She put her hand on his chest, and kept it there, and finally felt the slow rise and fall of breathing. She frowned, puzzled.

"I thought he had stopped having these spells. No one has mentioned it for quite a long while."

"I thought so, too. I came in to see about him, and found him like this. I'll stand by and keep a watch over him. He'll probably come out of it and sleep hard for hours. They don't seem to do him harm."

"But you heard him cry?"

"Cry?" Celta stared at Mildred. "That baby has never cried in his life that I ever heard."

"But I just now heard him. Distinctly. That's why I came in."

Celta shook her head firmly. "I've been here for almost an hour, and he hasn't uttered a sound."

A sudden movement in the crib drew their attention. The baby's eyes were closed now, and he yawned, drew his arms close to his body, turned slightly in the blankets and slept soundly. Color returned to his cheeks, and warmth. Mildred touched him, and he was undisturbed by it. She let her fingers linger against the soft, smooth warmth of his face.

"How often does he have these limp spells now, Celta?"

"He hasn't had any since Louise left. I'd know. When I took care of him right after he was born, before that Miss Duncan came, he had a few. And he had one while she was here, for she called downstairs about it. But I thought he had stopped altogether, until tonight."

"And you didn't hear anything? Had you been asleep?"

"No. I'd been reading. I couldn't sleep. I don't know why I decided to check on him. Then I just stood by, because nothing ever happens to him in these spells except what you saw. I didn't see any reason to disturb you."

Mildred drew away. "Perhaps I should have a doctor look in on him." Strange, how sure she had been that the cries were Jeremy's. But it hadn't been. Whatever it had been, it was gone now. "Goodnight, Celta. Why don't you go on to bed? I think he's sleeping normally. I'll call the doctor tomorrow."

She returned to her room, closing the door behind her. The night was comfortingly silent. She went back to bed and to an uninterrupted sleep.

The next day it rained again. Mildred went downstairs to her office and called the doctor. He would come tomorrow. Then she sat back a moment. She wanted to escape from everything for a while. Now that Celta had taken over with Jeremy, she was free to travel, to go wherever she chose. Provided the doctor's visit revealed nothing serious. And she didn't think it would. She had only to decide her route. She took the World Atlas back upstairs and locked herself into her suite.

She called travel agencies and airports and hotels, feeling her way toward unknown countries a bit cautiously.

Not until night had fallen again did she remember about the lost creature in the woods. She had forgotten to tell Clint to look for it, and now it was much too late; Clint had left hours ago. Mildred yawned. As soon as the doctor left, she would pack a few things and leave for New York for a few days. She could decide there on her itinerary abroad. At least in New York city there would be no abandoned animals crying in the woods.

As though her thought of it was awakening and disturbing to the creature itself, as though remembrance urged it forward, the first whine, the first sob of the dark night, came from beyond her window, her wall. Her body tensed.

The crying rose, the vowels forming. It seemed almost to be wailing the word *mama* in a weakening, dying way that Mildred could no longer stand. The temperature had dropped to freezing, and ice would be forming on every leaf, and perhaps even on that small animal's coat, over his skinny ribs. The thought made Mildred oddly angry. What had happened to the thing's mother? Had some trespasser, some poaching hunter, killed her? No mother abandoned her young willingly. The thought made her furious. Felicia was not abandoned. She was with her father.

Mildred got out of bed, found house shoes that came up past the ankle and were lined with something thick and furry, and the heaviest robe in the closet. From a desk drawer in her sitting room she took a flashlight and a small handgun. She stared at the gun, hearing the soft crying grow softer and farther away. The gun had been in that desk for years, with its small bullets in their little holes. There was something reassuring about it, and she needed reassurance, for the thought of going alone into the dark woods in search of whatever it was that cried, was deeply frightening. She hesitated, and thought about not going. But the cry was intolerable. It must be ended.

*Odd how it had seemed to be Jeremy last night.*

To make sure now that it was not Jeremy she opened the door to the nursery, but the dimly lighted room was silent. She glanced in. The crib was in shadow, and tonight Celta was not there beside it. Mildred went on down the hall and glanced in at the nurse's bedroom, and saw that Celta was in bed and had fallen asleep with a magazine in her hands, her glasses sliding down her nose, her mouth hanging open. She was propped up into a half-sitting position by two thick pillows behind her back. The lamp on the bedside table cast a bright circle over the pages of the magazine and the bony, vein-lined hands.

Mildred smiled faintly and closed the door.

The main hall was softly lighted, and Mildred passed through it swiftly, and down the stairway to the lower hall. She went out the back door, leaving it unlocked. On the terrace she paused to listen. There was no cry.

Wind rustled frozen leaves. Star points glowed brilliantly in a black sky without shedding any light earthward. A faint shadow fell before her from the hall light inside the glass door at her back. Ahead of her was total blackness, it seemed, until her eyes adjusted and separated tree tops from sky, and brick wall from the silent forest depths.

She stood waiting, listening, growing colder by the moment. Stiff fingers tugged the fuzzy neck of her robe closer, then slipped into the deep pocket where the small gun lay heavily against her thigh. Her other hand seemed frozen to the flashlight, and she thought about returning to the hall for gloves and old fur coat.

She moved at last to turn back into the house for warmth, and the wailing began, rising and falling softly in the still night, its melancholy cry stirring to silence an old hoot owl across the river, and bringing a wave of chills racing over Mildred's body. She felt oddly defenseless, and in danger. She recognized a rising sense of terror, something she had never felt before in her life.

That was ridiculous, she told herself firmly. This was a baby animal suffering in the woods. Even if it were a baby wildcat, there was no danger to her. It was simply lost from its mother, and cold and freezing, and hungry.

She snapped on the flashlight and, before she should lose all her nerve, hurried toward the woods and the soft cry. It came from just beyond the brick wall that separated the lawn from the forest, just to the left of the wood gate in that wall. It was probably huddled against the wall for shelter.

She passed through the gate and found it was coming from a bit farther on into the forest, moaning softly now, a certain eagerness in its voice as though it saw her coming and was not afraid of her, but wanted her. The cry dropped to a whimper of welcome that made her sorry for what she had to do. She swept the flashlight in an arc, and a touch of blue-white flashed somewhere to the left. She swung the flashlight back slowly, and found it.

*Jeremy.*

He sat in the leaves, dressed in white diaper and short white nightgown. His dimpled knees were bent slightly outward, his small feet entirely bare. His arms were lifted toward her, his hands reaching.

She felt a thrust of shock as cold as the air in these dark woods, and a swift bafflement. *What was Jeremy doing here?* But the eagerness on his face, the twisted misery and unhappiness mingled with delight, drew her with its needs. As she started toward him she felt a chilling prick of warning, a band of tightness go around her head to turn her back, to draw her away; but she ignored it. He was reaching for her and he needed her.

She went down on her knees in front of him, and he leaned forward, stretching upward, his hands reaching for her face. She laid the flashlight on the ground beside her knees, and started to speak, to reassure him, to tell him that she had come and would take care of him, but her thoughts were overpowered by the mystery of how he had come to be here in the woods alone. The beam of the flashlight sank into the dead leaves of the forest floor, and the other light, the faint blue glow, seemed to be increasing, and even as Mildred leaned closer to Jeremy, she paused, hesitated and drew back slightly. The blue light was coming from behind him, and as she stared she froze in horror, on her knees, her hands out to take him, for he was rising slowly away from the ground, as though by the power of the pale blue glow; and the lower part of his body was becoming elongated and rounded, trailing behind and beneath him like a tail ... curling and twisting and pushing him upward in its venomous and eerie blue, until from the hips down he had become reptilian ... like the snakes that had writhed and struggled together on the road so long ago, those snakes with their strange flattened heads and the bluish tinge of their bodies ...

Mildred was incapable of movement, of saving herself.

His hands reached her face and she felt the painful thrust of his thumbs into her eyes. She was blinded, and wild with pain. She felt the hot blood run down her face, and her hands lifted in defense, and found nothing but the twisting, slippery serpent body, writhing in her hands and curling around her neck, its tail searching for and finding her mouth as she tried to scream. She was being choked ... not strangled as Janet Duncan had been, but choked and gagged by the thing that had entered her mouth and was feeling its obscene way into her throat ... She fell sideways, fighting helplessly, feeling with her weakening fingers the slashes in her skin as his appendages ripped flesh from bone. Yet strangely she was now thinking with sharp, clear perception in these last minutes of her life, as though in her death struggles her brain sought and found answers. She knew now why Janet Duncan had tried to run. Janet had known ... she had seen. And she had died. Mildred knew now that Jeremy's origin lay in a mystery, a horror far more unbelievable even than Celta would be able to accept, far beyond Felicia's ability to remember. There had been no boy, there had been nothing human. She had not talked of his conception because she could not face the memory, for something more horrible than death had happened to her. *Felicia ... forgive me for not helping you ... forgive me.*

She had one last vivid thought before she lost consciousness: *I love you so, Felicia. Stay away.*

CELTA WOKE ABRUPTLY. Her light was still burning, her glasses almost falling off her nose. She sat forward, pushed her glasses back into place, put the magazine on the table. For a moment then she listened intently. Had there been a noise? The house seemed to be wrapped in silence now. She woke, she decided, because the magazine had slipped.

She yawned widely and deeply, swung her legs out of the bed, and rubbed her back. It was aching from the hours propped against two pillows. She flexed her toes. She listened again, and then checked the time. *Lord a'mercy, almost three o'clock.*

She went silently toward the nursery. He never seemed to need night care, but she'd rest better if she checked on him. She hoped he wasn't having another one of his spells. There was something unnerving about those spells, something she couldn't put her finger on, as though she sensed he was playing some kind of trick on her. They didn't seem to hurt him, at least. It was a lot of nonsense that the doctor was coming. If it was up to her, she wouldn't bother.

She stared down into the crib, and frowned. Again, as last night, his eyes were half-opened and staring upward blindly, his body limp. He seemed not to be breathing at all, and for a moment she thought he might have died, but his skin was faintly warm, and his pulse weak but even.

Celta watched him a moment, rubbing her hand unconsciously across her mouth, back and forth, back and forth. She had felt many times during his life that both Mildred and Felicia would be better off if the baby were gone, but it was not up to her to let him die. She was sure the spells were not dangerous to his health, but it really was up to Mildred to make that decision. If he was going to be having these spells every night, maybe Mildred ought to know.

Celta grasped the baby around the middle and shook him, but with no result. She checked his pulse again, and found it the same as before. With a grunt she made up her mind, and headed down the hall to Mildred's room.

The door stood open, the lights on inside. Celta moved into the room.

"Mildred?"

There was no answer. The bed was rumpled, the blankets thrown back, travel folders and notebooks scattered beside it. The dressing room was dark. Celta went on into the sitting room. The lights there were out. She went back into the bedroom and stood gazing at the bed a moment, rubbing her hand across her mouth in puzzlement.

She went out into the wide hall above the open stairway. The house was silent, yet something throbbed in that silence, alerting something in Celta's brain, urging her on, hurrying her to search for Mildred.

At four o'clock she called Clint from the phone in the downstairs office.

"Sorry to disturb you, Clint, but I think you'd better come on out here. I can't find Mrs. Stewart anywhere. I've looked all over the house, and I've got a feeling something's wrong. I think we'd better look outside. She didn't take a car out that you know of, did she?"

"No. All the cars were in the garage when I left. I'll be there in a few minutes, Celta."

While she was waiting she ran back upstairs and looked in on the baby. Now he was sleeping, his eyes closed, no longer blind and staring like some mindless doll. She tucked the blankets more closely about his small body and left him. From her closet she got her long coat and galoshes. Before she had them buttoned Clint had arrived. She followed him out with her galoshes flopping wide like the broken black wings of a raven.

"I can't imagine where she could have gone on a night as cold as this," she said as she followed him across the terrace. "As far as I can tell there's no coat gone, nor shoes at all except some house shoes and that heavy dark blue robe from her closet. It's almost like she meant to go outside, but not very far. She might've took a walk around the yard, but if she had, she would've been back by now, surely."

"Surely," Clint agreed. "She didn't drive. None of the cars have been moved."

His arm flung out suddenly and stopped her. His voice was chopped off to silence, his body tense. He cupped a hand for a moment over the flashlight he carried, and Celta saw immediately what had caught his attention. Just over the brick wall, coming from the forest, was a soft yellow glow.

They watched in silence, waiting for the light to move, to come toward them, to sweep from its steady glow against the dark tree trunks. Finally Clint spoke again, his voice low.

"Must be something wrong out there. That light's not movin'."

Celta nodded as though he could see her. Together they began to walk, Clint's light flashing again on the ground before them, the eyes of both raised to the eerie glow in the trees.

They found her where she had fallen, the flashlight burning on and on at her side. Celta recognized the robe and the house shoes and the rings on her fingers. She recognized the shape of the fingers, the long, tapered nails, the soft pink polish. But it was not possible to recognize the torn face, the blood-matted hair, the hideously ripped throat.

Celta staggered away, her hands to her own face, pressing hard, rebelling against what she saw. The glow of the light into the trees became part of a nightmare that would live with her the rest of her life. Just before she lost consciousness, she heard Clint cry out, "My Lord, oh my Lord, what kind of animal did this?"

# CHAPTER 12

Jeremy was six months old on November 12, and Felicia spent that entire long evening, after school, making a kind of birthday cake. She had found a recipe in a magazine, and had painstakingly followed it from the creaming of the sugar into the flour to the pouring of the batter into the carefully greased and floured cake pans. From the living room came the sound of the television set, her only companion. Her dad hadn't come home for dinner at all; he never did on Friday nights. She didn't mind. The cake took up her time, her thoughts. She pretended that Jeremy would be eating the cake with her, that he was waiting in the other room for her, or sitting in a baby swing behind her, watching. She would put six candles on it. Tiny candles, because it was months she was counting. Of course Mama was there too, and — her humming stopped, her moment of happiness destroyed. She worked on in silence, making frosting from powdered sugar and cream. It took an extra-long time to beat out the tiny sugar lumps and to make it the right consistency to spread and then hang on to the uneven sides of the layer cake. She kept coming out with either too much sugar or too much cream. By the time the late movie had gone off, Felicia was yawning. She was suddenly too sleepy even to eat what she had so slowly created.

The birthday party came to an end.

LEONARD LET himself into the apartment at fifteen minutes until three. He moved quietly to avoid waking his daughter and was annoyed that he felt the need. So what if he woke her? She could always go back to sleep. Still, he stepped light through the hall to the kitchen where he found the light on and the cake in the middle of the small kitchen table. Six tiny blue candles staggered across the top, leaning in varying directions, set down in frosting too unsteady to clamp them firmly. The white frosting had dripped down and overrun one side of the plate; the top of the cake most definitely tilted southward.

Leonard smiled. She was a pretty good kid. Quiet, too sad. Not really in his way, except he felt obligated to come home during the night, seven nights a week, just to check on her. She always slept with two or three lights on; he couldn't break her of the habit. All the rest he hadn't really minded. Together they had gone grocery shopping in the beginning, but after the second week he had turned it all over to her. She was fifteen now, her birthday just a week past, but in many ways she acted at least eighteen.

Her mother hadn't even called her to wish her happy birthday.

A birthday card had arrived, of course. There had also been cards from other people at Tanglewood. Celta and Clint. A card from some boy in Jonesboro — Gary Appleby. Felicia'd tossed that letter aside; she'd said he was a "creepy crawler." The cards had reminded him of her coming birthday. He'd asked what she wanted, and after a long thoughtful moment she had said she wanted to go to Disneyland. Another surprise. So, they had gone to Disneyland. And he had seen her laugh a couple of times.

Why had she baked the cake? Was it a belated wish for herself? The phone rang, invading the quiet apartment with the sudden, irritating noise. He ran for the hallway. Who the hell was calling at three-thirty in the damned morning?

"Yeah?"

"Mr. Stewart? This is Clint Reilly, at Tanglewood. Sorry to wake you up, sir, but something has happened here ..."

Leonard calculated the time difference. It was five-thirty at Tanglewood. Even back in the hills, that was early. "Yeah?" he said again, frowning.

"Mrs. Stewart is dead, sir."

"Mrs. Stewart? *Mildred?*"

"Yes sir. We just found her. I've called the sheriff and I thought I should call you right away too, sir. Celta wasn't able. She's lying down. I called the doctor too, and he'll look at her. I think it's just the shock, and she'll be all right. I thought you'd want to know. Miss Felicia as next of kin, and you as her guardian, will have to make the funeral arrangements, I suppose. I thought you would want to break the news to Miss Felicia."

"Why yes. Of course. What happened, Clint?'

"We don't know for sure. It was some kind of animal in the woods."

"An animal in the woods! Mildred?"

"Yes, sir. We found her just on the other side of the wall at the back of the yard. She had gone out in her nightclothes, carrying a flashlight. Looked like a terrible struggle. Celta was with me. It was hard on Celta. It was a terrible sight to see."

Leonard found himself assimilating the news with disbelief. None of it seemed real. "But she's only thirty-nine."

"Yes, sir," Clint said.

Leonard realized that must be a blow for Clint as well, for he had been the chauffeur since Mildred was in her teens.

"You probably should call her brother too, Clint. Can you do that for me? You can find his number in her telephone book — on her desk in the office, or in her sitting room upstairs. I'll contact the other relatives when I get there. Or Martin will. We'll be on the first available flight before the day ends. Meantime, just go ahead and do what has to be done."

After the phone was back in its cradle, he stood as he was and stared at the wall. What would it mean for Felicia? Now there was no chance she would be going back to Tanglewood to stay. Unless, of course, Mildred's brother, Martin would agree to let Celta stay on as her guardian.

*The baby*. He had entirely forgotten the baby boy. What was his name? Whose responsibility was he. No. *Oh, Jesus Christ*.

He wasn't a procrastinator. Get on with it and get it over, that was his way of handling anything unpleasant. He headed now for Felicia's bedroom. Maybe he would find that the phone had wakened her. At her door, he knocked and called her name, and waited for an answer that didn't come. He opened the door.

Three lights were on in the bedroom, one at the bedside, and two on the dresser. The girl lay sprawled on top of her covers, her pajamas wrinkled up to her knees, the top gaping away from the bottom, white stomach showing in the light. She was sleeping like a baby, soundly, deeply. But when he touched her cheek she came up as though he had burned her, crying out in a soft animal whimper, scuttering away from him with eyes wild and wide in terror. Recognition came slowly, it seemed, while he stared at her. She trembled now; he didn't know what kind of move he should make toward her.

None, perhaps. There was no way to soften this blow.

"You'd better get up and get dressed and packed," he said. "I'm taking you home today."

The fading fear in her eyes was replaced by hope, as bright and shining as the stars. "Home? Back to Tanglewood?"

"Yes. Something has happened to your mother, Felicia. She was found dead early this morning. Clint just called me." He backed toward the door. "You'd better pack all your things, just in case. I'm going to call the airlines."

She was sitting in the middle of her bed, her hands clamped hard across her mouth, her large eyes staring at him over the edges of her hand. She was beginning to shake her head in denial. He stepped into the hall and closed the door and took a long breath of relief. At least that was over. He didn't want to watch her cry.

CELTA SAT ON A STRAIGHT-BACKED CHAIR, one elbow on the kitchen table, while the doctor took her blood pressure. Beyond the windows she saw the rising sun slant bright, warm rays across the terrace and onto the brick wall at the edge of the forest. Seeing the sunshine reminded her just how long she had been sitting here in the kitchen while others moved about, while the sheriff had come and the ambulance, and the coroner. While the strange doctor listened to her heart and took her blood pressure.

He folded his equipment away and moved back. "You'd better get to bed, Mrs ..."

"Miss," Celta said.

"Miss ...?"

"Celta." She rolled her sleeve down.

"Miss Celta, you'd better go home and go to bed and try not to worry. Stay in bed for a couple of days. I can give you a few days' supply of something to relax you."

"No, I don't want it, thanks just the same. And this is my home. And I can't go to bed. I have to get upstairs and see about the bairn."

"The ... *bairn*?"

One of the maids had arrived for work, and now stood timidly against a kitchen counter watching Celta and the doctor. Her eyes showed her stunned disbelief at the news she had met on her arrival. Now she didn't know what to do, except to stand and wait.

She said softly, automatically, "Baby."

The doctor, an elderly man, looked even more surprised. "There's a baby?"

The young maid answered, "Yes sir. Mrs. Stewart's son, Jeremy. He's six months old."

"I didn't know. Hadn't heard about him. What a shame. Who'll be taking care of him now?"

"I will," Celta said sharply, rising from her chair, feeling a sudden dizziness that made her sway and clutch the edge of the table. When the Doctor made a move toward her she motioned him away. "I'll be all right. I'm going upstairs now, Imogene. You'd better get on with your work. Thank you, doctor, for coming out, but you didn't need to. Just send your bill here to Tanglewood. I'll take care of it at the end of the month."

She went slowly through the quiet halls, not comforted by the solitude. When she passed the grandfather clock and saw that it was past seven, a rise of anxiety prodded her into a quicker step. It had been hours since she had looked in on Jeremy. He would be awake now, and wet and hungry. She helped herself upstairs by grasping the handrail in fingers that seemed to have lost most of their strength. She dared not think what would happen if another of the dizzy spells came and wiped her off her feet. It was with a sense of accomplishment that she reached the upper hallway. She went along it soundlessly toward the nursery.

Jeremy was still asleep, just as she had seen him last at three o'clock. He didn't look as though he had moved at all. His blankets were still tucked around him, leaving only his head free.

She turned away, went into the nursery bedroom, and lay down across the bed. Her eye closed, but there was no rest, no real relaxation. Images danced behind her eyelids, from the terrible scene in the woods to the nursery, from one to the other, back and forth, as though they were in some way connected. On the periphery wavered Felicia. She would be coming home now. Clint had called Mr. Stewart, he said. Celta's feelings about Felicia coming home were mixed. She was both glad and fearful. Somehow, even in his physical helplessness, that strange bairn had something to do with Mildred's death. She was sure of it. Why Mildred? Celta did not know. But now her fears for Felicia were growing stronger until anxiety speeded her heart and forced her fluttering eyelids open.

She lay still, looking up at the ceiling.

FELICIA BEGAN TREMBLING UNCONTROLLABLY when her father helped her out of the taxi in front of Tanglewood. In one hand she carried a soft squeezable, fuzzy little stuffed animal she had found at the air terminal gift shop in Los Angeles. On the way home she had held it against her cheek for hours, and found in it a kind of comfort that nothing else gave her.

Leonard asked, leaning down toward her, "Are you cold?"

"Yes," she answered, her teeth chattering audibly when she spoke, but it was more than cold. Far more. And her father seemed to understand.

He said, "You'd better go straight up to bed, and if you don't get to feeling better, call me, and I'll bring a doctor to look in on you."

She nodded. She didn't tell him that she was going straight to the nursery, not to bed. She was going to hold her baby, at last, forever.

Someone opened the door for them; Felicia noticed only that it was not Celta. Her eyes moved instantly upward toward the head of the stairs. The nursery door was not visible from here, but she knew exactly at what point it so silently beckoned. She began to run, up the stairs, carrying the stuffed toy and the overnight case.

She dropped her overnight case outside the nursery door so that she could turn the knob, and left it there, forgotten. He was on his hands and knees when she saw him, his eager eyes watching the door as though he knew she was coming. At the side of the crib she dropped the toy as well, and it fell and bounced and rolled to one side. Jeremy was reaching his arms out for her, sitting back so that both arms were raised, his throat giving forth a low moan of welcome, almost of sobs. Felicia pulled him over the side of the crib and enclosed him in her arms. He clutched her with both hands, whimpering like a little animal overcome by emotion, rubbing his head against hers.

"Oh my baby, Jeremy! I'm so glad to see you, so glad! You've grown so much. You're so heavy now." She tried to hold him away so that she could look at him, but he clung to her, hands clutching hard on her coat shoulders, arms stronger than would seem possible. She hugged him, kissed him, kissed him again and again.

She looked over his head and saw that Celta was standing just inside the bedroom door, watching them. Her lined, aged face sagged with grief. "Celta! He's so glad to see me, Celta."

"Yes."

It seemed for a moment that Celta would cry, but then her face went back to a semblance of composure.

"And I'm so glad to see him," Felicia murmured, kissing him again, leaving her lips against the side of his forehead. "It's been so long. Such a long time."

"It can seem long," Celta said. "When you're so young."

"You look so tired, Celta. Please go on to bed, and I'll keep Jeremy. I'll take care of him. I'll feed him his supper."

"No, he's my job. I'll go to bed when I've got him settled for the night."

"You can at least go down and eat your dinner in peace, and let me keep him until you're ready to settle him in."

"I reckon I could do that." She came to Felicia, patted her back for a moment. "I'm glad to see you, too, Felicia. Same as the bairn."

Felicia couldn't answer. She could only try to smile at Celta, and caution herself in silence again: *I will not think of Mama ... being gone forever. I will not think of that. Mama has gone to Europe, and she wanted me to come home and stay. She loved me after all. I will think only of my little baby boy ... and he's so big now, twice as big, it seems, but he hasn't really changed. He hasn't forgotten me at all.*

She bent with an effort to the floor, Jeremy heavy in her arms, and picked up the little toy. She sat down in the rocking chair, and the baby relaxed against her, his round bottom warm in her lap, his head against her breast. She talked to him of the toy, and his fingers tugged at the fuzzy, limp little ears and picked at the bead eyes.

She held him, rocked him, and let the darkness come.

Celta came back and turned on the light. "You asleep?" Celta asked.

"No. Just sitting here. He's so quiet. He likes me to hold him."

"You'd better go on now and get your own dinner, and your rest. You'll be needing it. Your Uncle Martin has arrived. And some other relatives."

"Uncle — ? Yes. I hardly know him."

She handed Jeremy to Celta, kissed him again. He reached for her; she promised to return. Without looking back she left the room. If she looked at him, if she saw again his yearning, she would not be able to leave and go among the people who would be talking of her mother's death. Only in the nursery, with Jeremy, was she safe and loved. With him there were lullabies, and picture books, and nursery rhymes. Beyond his door were people she had never seen in her life. And death.

She went first to her room, and bathed and dressed. As she started to leave, the old strangling fear returned, the fear of the dark and of the unknown, unfathomable things it held. She went back into her room and turned on the bedside lamp, and the lamp on the dressing table, leaving them burning behind her.

Dinner was in the large, formal dining room, even though most of the people had not dressed for it. This room, this expanded table, was the only one large enough to hold all of them. Felicia recognized Uncle Martin, broad-bodied, exuding power. She lost track immediately of those who introduced themselves to her, so that she forgot if they were great-aunts of her mother, or just third cousins. She didn't know if the men were the relatives, or were married to relatives. As soon as she decently could after dinner, she left them.

She found Jeremy asleep, and Celta already in her own bed, a magazine resting against her stomach and her head drooping over it. Careful to disturb neither of them, Felicia went on into the quiet dark halls.

She closed and locked her door, and with her own lights still burning went to bed. She was suddenly very, very tired, and sleep came quickly.

The sound woke her within minutes, feeling heavy and drugged and only half-conscious. Something was outside her door, scratching lightly, reminding her of her little dog of years ago, so that at first she thought it was Timmy again, and she got up while still half-asleep to let him in. At the door she touched the knob, and as though the little dog had seen her through the solid wood and had stopped his scratching to wag his tail, the sound was gone, and only waiting silence remained. And suddenly the warning chills were over her body, moving down her throat and onto her arms and chest, crying out to her, *don't open that door.*

She stood very still, cold in her pajamas. There was no sound at all from the other side of the door, from the dark side.

It began again, softly, moving now against the door, brushing, becoming faster, faster, impatient, angry. Felicia began backing away, terror closing her throat. What would she find if she opened the door? If she stepped into the darkness, that sunless, lightless world that was his only pathway? Had he achieved shape now, and form?

The movement outside the door paused, and then a tender young voice said, "Mama? Mama?"

Felicia screamed silently and covered her ears with her hands. She ran to her bed and covered herself completely in the blankets and held her ears against the call that could *not possibly, not possibly be from her own baby boy.*

Tomorrow night, and all the nights from now on, she would leave the lights on all along the hallway, and she would rise at two o'clock, just as she used to, and go to the nursery and hold and rock her baby. But tonight she would not open the door.

MANY PEOPLE from Jonesboro gathered at the Presbyterian church for the funeral of Mildred Marchant Stewart. Few of them were intimately acquainted with any Marchant, but all of them felt a certain kinship. The Marchant family was Jonesboro's elite. The bank, and several businesses, and various other real estate was owned by the Marchant family. It was all theoretically run by Martin Marchant, that elusive man who had left Jonesboro early in life, first for private schools when he was a boy, then for business headquarters and home in New York now that he was a man. At one time he had gone to school in Jonesboro, and there were some who remembered him as an old playmate. He did not remember them. So they gathered on the winter-brown lawn of the large white brick church, and talked quietly among themselves about the Marchant family.

It was the older Marchants who had belonged to the church, said some of the elderly people who should know. It was the old grandmother, Mary Jane Marchant. She was the real, the stable, member of the family and the town. Mary Jane had been a Clowinger, you know, before she married Phillip Marchant. Mary Jane and Phillip had two sons, and both of them were killed during World War Two. Paul was the only one who married and had children. He married Coleen Gray, from South Carolina. They just had two children, Mildred and Martin, and Mildred married someone she met in college: Stewart? Of course, Leonard Stewart. Mildred's daughter, Felicia, was named Felicia Jane Stewart, and she went to school with the other Jonesboro children until last year, when she was taken out for some reason and sent to private schools. No matter how you looked at it, the Marchants kept to themselves in a way, for even after Felicia went away she didn't so much as write a card to anyone. Strange. Yes, the rich are different.

Mildred was killed by an animal, they said. What kind of animal do you suppose would do that? We don't have bears in our woods most of the time, and are bears that vicious? Grizzlies might be ... didn't you hear about the grizzlies in the Rocky Mountains attacking and killing those students? But we don't have grizzlies here. A posse of sorts went searching through the woods after it happened, my husband was on it, and nothing was there except a few raccoons, squirrels, and chipmunks. Not even a wildcat. Well, but those creatures would hide during the day, wouldn't they? No matter, I don't intend to take any walks in that direction. What do you suppose they will do with the girl, Felicia? Just send her back to school? Of course, there's her father ... I almost forgot him. They're divorced now, you know. Mildred and Leonard. Well Felicia's fifteen now, the same age as my girl. But there's a baby, you know ...

A baby!

Didn't you know? Mildred Marchant had a baby. It must be several months old by now. Louise Madson worked out there and took care of that baby for a while, and did you see her when she quit? Her eyes were black and blue and her face was scratched, and she said the baby poked her in the eye with his thumbs! More than likely she had a fight with her boyfriend, Rob Farmer. You remember him ... from Evansburg. He's the one got in that fight with those boys from Mountain. Of course that was when he was younger, and kind of macho, but you know people never really change from their basic nature! He probably poked her.

Laughter, soft, subdued, stifled.

The crowd parted, creating a pathway from the street to the church door as the black limousine drew to a quiet stop at the curb, and the black chauffeur, Clint Reilly, dressed in dark uniform, got out and opened the wide back door. The family emerged from the car and gathered for a moment before going up the walk into the church. Behind the limousine other cars drew in, some of them with New York and other out-of-state license plates, all with unfamiliar passengers.

Martin Marchant, dressed in black, led the way, his hawk-like face looking straight ahead. Just slightly behind him came Felicia, her hand on Leonard Stewart's arm. Her face too was set and unemotional, masklike. Her long hair glistened in the bright November sunlight. She wore a black suit, but at her throat was a soft coral scarf, the only touch of color. All the other people, cousins, great-aunts, distant and strange, did not interest Jonesboro. The residents had come to pay homage to Mildred Marchant, to her brother and her daughter, and one by one they filed into the church until it was packed, standing room only, while others continued to stand on the lawn and discuss family history, going back to the settlement of the country when the original Marchant had arrived from Europe and gathered unto himself all the land he could possibly handle. They discussed the changes from the old days to now, when a large family had dwindled down to one daughter now surviving ... no, there also was a son, someone said. And of course there was also Martin Marchant, but he no longer was really a part of Tanglewood and Jonesboro. There was only the daughter, Felicia. And of course the other one, the infant son. Interesting, wasn't it, that the more the family dwindled the more reclusive they became, so that now they were beginning to keep entirely to themselves?

Strangers among us.

FELICIA WAS RELIEVED that the casket was closed and would remain closed. She could not bear to see her mother lying there. She wanted to think of her as having taken that trip to Europe, just as she had wanted. And oh God, why hadn't she? If only time could be turned back to August, and she could persuade her mother to go on to Europe, she would be alive now.

But of course that's where she was, Europe, she was! This other thing, this church full of people all sad and serious, these strangers, these relatives were not really there. Think of good things ... Jeremy ... Jeremy, so sweet, but grown so much! Such a big baby boy now, so husky.

There were some in the church whose eyes were on Felicia at the moment the faint, gentle smile curved her lips; and they were horrified. And they discussed it later until the rumor had snaked its way through all the town. The girl had sat smiling during her mother's funeral.

Strange people, the Marchants. Yes, it seemed to be getting that way.

CELTA WATCHED JEREMY IN AMAZEMENT. He had pulled himself up at the side of the crib and, holding with one plump hand, was reaching the other toward her, stretching upward, standing tiptoed. A wide smile rounded his mouth. For the first time in his life he seemed eager for her to pick him up. He was partly cooing, partly laughing. Laughing right out loud.

She felt herself melting, responding. He was laughing out loud, and he was acting like any normal baby. Could she have been wrong about him after all? For didn't everyone know that changelings did not laugh out loud? If they could be made to do so, they would instantly change back to their original form, which of course was neither human nor animal, but something horrible, something unknown from those dark places of perpetual night. Had she been wrong?

She stood in the middle of the nursery and watched him. She was alone in the house with Jeremy. Someone had to stay with the baby while the funeral was in progress, and she had chosen to stay for a number of reasons. For one, she didn't trust anyone else with the baby, or, more correctly, she didn't trust him with any of the maids. And also, she couldn't bear to go to Mildred's funeral. She had come nearer being her daughter than anyone else in the world.

Mildred would understand.

Celta wondered at the change in him. He had slept and slept the day that Mildred was found. He had slept as though exhausted from some great effort. He had slept so hard and so long that she had become concerned about it, and then had thought it would be a blessing if he would continue to sleep and never wake up. But finally, a little before Felicia came into the nursery, Jeremy had awakened. Even now, thinking of it, tears dampened Celta's eyes, for she had never seen anything so touching in her life. The baby had raised himself, lifted his arms to Felicia, and then had clung to her and clung to her, rubbing his head against her almost like a cat, loving her, holding her, whimpering. Yes, actually whimpering. Celta had been deeply touched at their happiness in being together again.

That was when the change had come. And now the thought sobered her, and almost frightened her.

Was it an example of the power of mother love?

Or was it something more?

"What are you wanting?" Celta asked amiably as she came closer to the crib. "You can't be hungry yet, and you're good and dry." She met his reaching hand with hers, and felt his fingers close and tighten and tug her toward him.

For a moment she held back, then she gave in, her smile deepening, and lifted him out of the crib. She found herself holding him close in her arms, feeling his weight against her chest. His small right arm half encircled her neck, almost affectionately it seemed, while his other hand went to his mouth. He made sounds around his fist, baby sounds.

"Want to sit and rock a while?" Celta asked, finding him too heavy to carry for very long, for arms as old as her own. She spoke her thoughts aloud: "Takes young arms to carry a bairn that's getting as chunky as you, young arms like your mama's — "

She realized what she had said and stopped too late. She had given Mildred her word that no one would ever hear the truth of Jeremy's birth from her. And no one meant Jeremy as well as all the others.

She'd have to watch her tongue.

Holding him on her lap she sat in the rocking chair, and sunlight fell warmly through the window upon them. Jeremy tilted his face up and looked at Celta, and her eyes met his in long, steady gaze. She noticed for the first time the unusual blue of his eyes, almost black turquoise with paler flecks of depth and endlessness, as though she looked into a distant place through glass. They were oddly beautiful. He was staring so intently into her face that she became uneasy. His wide baby smile was gone. The thin, dark, winged brows above his eyes had edged more closely together, raising a tiny bump of a frown; his moist little mouth drooped in a narrow pout. He was searching her, it seemed, invading her mind for something of importance to himself only.

The small face changed suddenly. The frown was gone, the mouth began widening in a grin, and again he was reaching up for her, both hands touching and caressing her creased and wrinkled cheeks.

Celta smiled, pleased despite herself, and did not move back from his touch.

# CHAPTER 13

The fate of the family was being decided. As it affected not only Felicia, but Celta, too, both of them were in the library with Leonard Stewart and Martin Marchant. Celta sat on a straight-backed chair as stiffly as though she wore an eighteenth-century corset. She had never been close to Martin. When she had come to work for the Marchant family her job was to take care of one-month-old Mildred. Martin was already fifteen years old and away at school most of the time. He had treated her like a servant. She had known of his two divorces, his travels, his childishness. Celta listened politely, keeping her thoughts to herself.

Felicia sat on one end of the leather divan, as stiffly as Celta. Her feet were straight and close together, her knees pressed tight. She looked at her hands in her lap. Behind the huge desk her uncle Martin leaned in the chair with the spring seat that groaned and complained rustily with his every move. He seemed unaware of the sounds.

At the windows overlooking the valley, the road, and the river; Leonard Stewart stood looking out. He had his hands stuffed into his pockets, and his fingers jiggled something there. Felicia sensed his desire to hurry with this and leave. Several days had passed now since they had left Los Angeles, since he had attended to his business and his private life. Felicia felt he would be leaving her behind, felt he was glad of that fact. But exactly where she was going was not yet established.

Martin said, "It's an interesting and puzzling fact that Mildred's will not only did not provide a dime for her son, Jeremy, but does not in any way mention him. The trust for Felicia includes almost everything she owned, and after her bequest to Celta nothing remains for him." Celta was to have fifteen thousand dollars a year for the remainder of her life. Martin went on: "Her heir is stated specifically as Felicia. There's no opening for any other heir."

Leonard said, "She just hadn't updated her will obviously."

"Yes, obviously. So that puts him entirely in your care, Leonard. Now that she's dead, you have custody, without a doubt. You'll be taking him with you?"

Leonard turned slowly from the window and stared. He had been left out in the cold along with Jeremy. The will was dated after their divorce, but before Jeremy's birth.

"My care," Leonard said thoughtfully and with growing anger. This was something he just hadn't thought about. His mind had been on getting the funeral business over, settling Felicia in a school somewhere, and leaving. *Leaving.* He wanted the freedom that he had just started to find in California before Felicia was thrust on him.

Martin said, with a twisted little smile of sarcasm, "He is your son, Leo, after all. What else should we do with him? Of course, it's your choice."

Leonard looked at Felicia. She had raised her face toward him, toward the window behind him. The light revealed strain and waiting fear. Was she afraid of what he was going to say? Was the truth a source of shame for her? Not once had she mentioned the child to him. He had no idea of her feelings toward him. Still, he had himself to think about, too. He made a good living, but not a great one. He no longer had to support Felicia, which added to the possibility of his own pleasure and comfort, and he certainly didn't want to be the main support of a child he hadn't even seen. Although he had been at Tanglewood almost a week now, it hadn't occurred to him to go up to the nursery.

Celta was looking at him also, accusingly. He avoided her eyes.

"The boy isn't mine," he said softly, almost guiltily.

The room, for a moment, was as quiet as though sound had ceased to exist. Then Martin snorted in derision.

"Come on now, Leo, don't try to tell me that dear strait-laced Mildred got him somewhere else. I won't buy that. In these modern times my sister was a phenomenon of old-fashioned virtues and beliefs. I can't see her getting pregnant elsewhere — unless she was raped."

Felicia said suddenly, "He's mine."

Martin stared at his niece as though he hadn't seen her before. His eyes went swiftly from her face to her feet, and away, back to Leonard again. "Is this true?"

"There's no reason for her to lie to you," Leonard said flatly.

"No. I'm sorry. It was just that the thought hadn't once occurred to me. After all, she's only a child herself. Well, a young girl. What are you, Felicia, fourteen?"

"Fifteen."

"And how old is the baby?"

"Six months."

Martin stared thoughtfully at the wall a moment. "No wonder Mildred never mentioned him to me, or in her will. He was undoubtedly an embarrassment to her. Of course, she had no idea that her death would take place so soon. What did she have in mind for the boy, does anyone know ?"

Celta said, "She was raising him as her own, sir. And the only reason he wasn't mentioned in her will was as Mr. Stewart said — she hadn't got round to it. She had other things on her mind. She told me herself that she intended for him to spend his life here at Tanglewood, protected from the world."

'Why would she want to protect him from the world?"

"He wasn't a normal bairn."

Martin gazed almost blankly at Celta. He hadn't seen the baby boy but had simply assumed, after the surprise of hearing of his existence, that he was like any other. "How is he not normal, Celta? Just tell me without being prodded every step of the way, as though you don't want to talk about it at all. No one here is going to repeat anything you have to say."

Celta hesitated a brief moment. "The doctor thought he might be retarded. I thought he ... was different. He never cried nor made a sound until lately. I mean to say, he still has never cried. But he's beginning to coo and go on like he ought to, so I reckon he's coming along better than the doctor expected."

"Well, it sounds more to me like the boy will have to be institutionalized, now that Mildred isn't here to keep the place together. What I had in mind was closing the house, keeping Clint on as caretaker, and I suppose Celta can go back to the old country, or get herself a small place in town. Felicia, of course, can go away to school. My attorneys can find a good place for the boy ... Is that all right with you, Leonard?"

"Fine with me. Not that I have any say over anything anyway."

"Felicia is yours, and since the boy is hers, that rather puts you in the driver's seat. Along with my attorneys, of course, since I'm the trustee."

"It sounds sensible to me. I have a plane to catch, and a small business of my own to get back to." He checked his watch, as though he had to leave within minutes.

Felicia had gotten to her feet, ignored by the men, trembling with fear of the power these men held over her life, over the life of her baby. "I object," she said firmly.

All eyes turned upon her in varying states of surprise. No one challenged her.

"My mother left me a monthly income, didn't she? And when I'm twenty-one I'll get half of the principal, and the rest will remain in trust for my heirs, won't it? And my mother's holdings were figured to be close to four million dollars, right? Well, I may not be of age yet, but why can't I make a few decisions? Jeremy is mine. There's no longer any reason to pretend he isn't. It was Mother who was ashamed of him, and of me for having him, not me. He's the most precious baby on earth, and I want to raise him myself. And this house, Tanglewood, was mother's, so therefore, it's now mine. Isn't it?"

Martin looked at Leonard, smiled slightly, and turned his eyes back to Felicia in amusement. "Yes," he said. "Now what do you have in mind, Felicia?"

"I want to stay here, and keep the house open, and raise my son here."

"Good Lord, you must be kidding!" Martin said. "A fifteen-year-old is not mature enough to take on that much responsibility."

"Celta would stay with me, wouldn't you, Celta?"

But even Celta was looking at her in astonishment, and remembering, remembering how fast Jeremy could change, how he could go from sweet and charming to severely cruel, scratching cheeks and eyes and yanking out hair. As he grew older ... stronger ...

"Absolutely not!" Leonard said, his narrow face turning a dull red, with anger, with frustration. He had hoped to get out of this without problems, but Felicia, that quiet daughter who had not mentioned her son one time during her stay with him, was now looking as though she would kill anyone who tried to separate her from him. And not even he, as much as he wanted freedom, was going to walk off and leave her in this huge old house, out here in the country where her own mother was killed by some strange animal ... "It would be insane for you to stay here, for anyone to stay here. Whatever it was that killed Mildred could very easily come down out of the hills and kill you, too. I won't allow it."

Felicia cried, "But that was ... that was ..."

Martin said, "Your dad's right, Felicia."

Felicia turned to Celta. "Please Celta! Help me." And there was that too. *The animal ... or whatever it had been.* There were so many dangers here now for Felicia.

Celta looked at her, saw the pleading in her eyes, the sparkle of tears, and knew she would stay with Felicia regardless of the dangers, or perhaps because of them, to try to ward them off ... but she hoped it wouldn't come to that. She hoped Felicia would listen to the men because they were right, far more right than they knew. "Felicia," Celta said slowly. "They're right. You should do as they say."

Felicia's body bent forward in frustration and unhappiness. Her hands clenched at her side. "You're all against me, all of you! But you, Celta, why?"

"They're right, Felicia. You'd be safer — "

"No! I won't listen to any more. I'm not going to let you do this to me, and to my baby! I won't have him put in a ... *place*! I won't! I'm not going to listen to you anymore."

She ran from the room crying openly now, a girl who hadn't cried for a long time, all the hurts pouring out from the shock of her pregnancy, to her mother's abandonment, and loss of the baby she had grown to love, to the death of her mother. All of it, mixed into unbearable stress, burst out at once. She ran blindly into the hall, up the stairs and on into the nursery. The bright room was a shimmer of colors, as though she looked at it from the bottom of a lake, and at its heart was her baby, sitting in his crib, reaching out for her.

She clutched him to her, arms enclosing him entirely, pressing him into the curves of her breasts, her neck. She fell into the corner of the room with him, burying her face against his soft body. She rocked on her buttocks, cradling him between her raised knees and her firm young bosom. Between deep, wrenching sobs she told him, "They're going to separate us again, Jeremy. They want to send us both to institutions — me to a terrible old school — you to something — an asylum — something — I don't think I can stop them, Jeremy. I don't think I can."

His hands twisted into her hair, clutching, pulling, but the pain it brought to her eyes was a welcome distraction from the pain and anguish in her heart. He was holding her to him, pulling her face even closer to his own so that cheek was flattened against cheek, and her tears wet his as well as her own. The sobs ended as he held her, as she whispered, "Don't, baby, you're hurting me."

As though he understood, his hold on her hair loosened and his arms went around her neck, tight, warm, desperate. Together they sat, huddled into the corner of the nursery, silent, unmoving.

"SHE SEEMS to feel very strongly about this," Martin said in a subdued tone of voice. The echoes of the girl's wailing had settled into the silence of the house, but none of the three in the library had moved or spoken.

"I didn't know she cared so much," Leonard said. "Maybe it would be all right for her to stay with him. If that's what she wants, why not?"

Martin looked at Celta. "Would you stay on here with her?"

None of them felt the tears and the heartache of the girl more than Celta. She sat in misery, wanting to go and comfort the child as she would have two years ago, but knowing that such comfort was not possible now. She could no longer say to her, *no matter, little girl, tomorrow it will all be gone, all the sadness, and the hurt, and you'll be happy and well again. Don't cry, little one, for it's only a small bruise, a little scratch, and it's hardly bleeding at all. Celta will make it well and color it all red with Mercurochrome.*

She said carefully, for these men would never believe her suspicions about the bairn, "I think it would be better for Felicia, when she has grown used to it, for her to leave here and go somewhere else to live. Perhaps back to California with Mr. Stewart, or to a good girls' school somewhere far away. This is not a happy place any more, not as it used to be. With her mother gone, she should go away, and stay away. The bairn will be cared for, by others, better than she could care for him, and — maybe — maybe — he will — forget her soon." Her eyes darted, searching, finding no way toward the real truth. What were his powers? What harm could he do others? Were there any real powers at all, or was it just an old woman's imagination?

Both men were staring at her as though trying to ferret out her reason for not staying with a girl she had helped rear. Was she so cold, so hard-hearted?

Martin said, "Then you want to retire, to get yourself a place of your own and live alone?" Celta looked down at her hands. They were shaking, and she clutched them together so the men wouldn't see. "I think that would be best if you want to close the house."

"I beg your pardon? I didn't understand you."

Celta raised her voice, and her head, and looked directly at Martin. "Yes, sir," she said.

"Then that's settled, for she certainly can't stay here without you. Finding another person like Celta would not be possible in these days, wouldn't you say so, Leonard?"

"I'd say so, yes."

"Then do you want to handle the placement of the children, or would you like my attorneys to do it?"

Leonard checked his watch again. "I really must leave. Will you make preliminary arrangements? But call me, please, before any final decision."

Martin nodded. "I'll get busy on it as soon as I get back to New York. I'm leaving today, too. Celta, you will stay on here until other arrangements can be made for the children? It should only take a week or so, maybe less."

Celta nodded her head, not trusting her voice.

When Celta entered the nursery Felicia was still huddled into the corner, her head down against the baby, her arms enclosing him protectively, and her face hidden. She had gone to sleep in that position, clutching her baby instinctively though she slept, exhausted by her fears. The baby, though, was not sleeping, his head was upright against his mother's, his arms tight around her neck.

Celta went to the rocking chair, and sat down. Beyond the window pane, frozen rain sleeted in tiny white drops, the only sound in the entire world it seemed, with its soft, pecking murmurs against the wall, the window, the dried winter grass and leaves.

Felicia needed the rest, Celta knew. Since her arrival every night after the first she had sat with the baby for long hours. Each morning Celta had found her drooping sleepily over the alert Jeremy, and told her to go to bed. And usually, Felicia wearily obeyed. But then later, if Celta herself woke and went to check on the baby, she found Felicia there again, the boy in her arms. "He'll just sleep the night away if you'll keep away from him," she said on one of those nights.

Felicia's answer had been rather odd. She said, "I wish he would!"

Celta eased back in the rocking chair, careful of the squeak it had developed lately. She didn't want to wake Felicia, even though the girl looked uncomfortable. Any sleep was better than none.

How soon would Martin make the arrangements for them? How long now before Felicia would be leaving forever?

*Would Felicia ever forgive her*?

Celta's dimming eyes moved toward Mildred's suite of rooms.

Their door was closed now, she knew. Its blank room, stark white, was as meaningful as the closed lid of the casket Celta had gone to see the night before the funeral. It marked an end to a life. It came closer to ending Celta's own life than anyone could know. Now she would be leaving this house and this family, and going to spend the rest of her days alone. And of her own decision, based on her own suspicions.

Was she wrong?

Jeremy seemed so different lately, since Felicia had come home, with not so much as a suggestion of the spells he once had, not at least that she saw.

A vision played itself against the white door suddenly. A dark forest, the golden glow of light splayed upwards against the bare branches, and at the edge of that light the hideously torn and bloodied face of Mildred. But now, as though her subconscious threw it abruptly to the surface, Celta saw another thing, something about that scene that she hadn't faced before. The eyes. Mildred's eyes. There were none. What had happened to her eyes? Where they should have been only deep, bloody holes remained.

Celta realized she was gripping the arms of the chair until her chest ached, and straining forward as though to understand this sudden sense of urgency.

She sat back in her chair, and forced relaxation of her arms to ease her chest.

*Louise ... Louise had quit her job as Jeremy's nurse because of his attack on her eyes.*

That was it, the elusive connection that had bothered her. But Jeremy could not have been the one to attack Mildred. She had seen him, herself, lying in his crib that night. And there was no way he could have left the crib. Unless, somehow, it happened during one of his spells. Perhaps it was during those strange, unconscious periods of his that he was most capable of evil.

The dark and vicious changelings, it was said in the old country, could leave their bodies at will and travel through the walls.

But did she really believe that was possible? Yes, but in spirit form only, and spirit form had no substance. It could neither feel nor be felt.

*I tell you, Mildred, there's something not right about that bairn. I'd watch him close if I was you. Better yet, I'd go ahead and let them take him away, for you never know what he will cause to happen. It's said the dark changelings never laugh and never cry, and can leave their bodies and travel wherever they want.*

*Celta, if you mention that nonsense to me again, I'll have them come and take you away! I have never heard such preposterous tales in my life! The baby is probably mute or something of that nature. Or perhaps he's just plain lazy and finds oral expression too much effort. I want to hear no more, Celta.*

And perhaps Mildred had been right. The baby had been slow in making sounds, but she had heard him laugh and respond to language. She had heard it herself.

So perhaps she had been wrong about him all along. Maybe she had done Felicia a great injustice by making that final decision on her future, by being the one who said it was better to take her away from her baby.

She looked at them, huddled back into the corner, their arms still tight around each other. Their positions had changed slightly, so that it looked as if the baby were holding the mother now, cradling her head against his chest as she slept.

His head was turning slowly, so very slowly that Celta felt waves of quiet horror move along her flesh from her neck to her ankles. She longed to look away, to get up and run from the room, but as though she stared at the slow-moving head of a poisonous snake she watched, waited, breath stilled. His eyes came toward her, glowing, those deep, turquoise flecks flashing a kind of fire as from the depths of cold space, and there was no human recognition, no friendliness, nothing but ancient hostility. Celta was held captive under the stare from those chilling eyes. But she knew finally, and positively, that she had not made the wrong decision about Felicia's future.

The sooner she was gotten away from that bairn, that creature, the safer she would be.

# CHAPTER 14

Felicia woke to the gentle caress of Jeremy's hand on her face. His arms were still warm around her neck. The sudden pleasure, the bitter-sweet happiness she felt in his closeness, was like being bathed in a rush of blossom-scented spring air.

She buried her face against Jeremy, rubbing back and forth like a kitten, his own little game turned, until he began to laugh. Deep in her throat she made a gurgling, growling sound that made the baby laugh all the harder and try to push his mother's head away.

She remembered abruptly what they were going do to her and Jeremy, and she grew still. Her head lifted, and she gazed blankly at the far wall. Jeremy grew still, watching her, seeing the faint frown between her eyebrows. His hand reached for her face again and patted, anxiously.

She said in a whisper, "They're going to separate us again, baby. Uncle Martin is going to find a private school for me, and a place for you, a terrible place where there are homeless, sick people. And there's nothing I can do that I've thought of, until I'm of age. And then they can't make me do anything anymore."

Her gaze came back to him and slowly roamed his head and face and even his hands and fingers. She leaned him against her knees and held a wrist in each hand, separating his fingers and examining them.

"You're beautiful, you're perfect. Maybe if I took you downstairs and made them look at you, get to know you, they'd change their minds and let us live together. I don't have to hide you now. Now that they know who you really are. I don't have to pretend any more that you're my baby brother. She slapped his palms together and laughing, said, "Patty cake, patty cake, come on and let your mommy dress you in your handsomest outfit!"

She put him into his crib while she rummaged through the chest drawers. She finally found a little blue and white knit romper with matching socks and caps, and began dressing his round little body. When he was dressed from cap to socks and shoes, she stood him on the floor and held his hands to keep him from falling. His legs were sturdy and straight, though plump and dimpled and it took only the slightest touch to keep him upright.

"Can you walk?" she asked, drawing her hand slightly away, forcing his fingertips to follow her.

He took an awkward step, and then another.

Felicia laughed in astonished delight.

"You can! You can!" She grabbed him up in her arms and ran with him from the nursery. "When they see that, they won't dare try to tell me my baby's not normal!"

At the bottom of the stairs she met Celta. The smile that came faintly to her lips did not spread to her eyes.

"Well, where are you going?" she asked.

"I've come to show Jeremy to Dad and Uncle Martin. And Celta, he can walk a little bit now, he really can! I want them to meet him, and see how beautiful he is, and all the things he can do. Neither one of them has even seen Jeremy, and once they do, I know they'll change their minds about him and — "

What little smile Celta had produced disappeared. She touched Felicia's elbow. "Felicia! Don't child. They've already left."

"Left! Where to? What for?"

"They've both gone home. They left while you were asleep."

"They can't have! They didn't even see him!"

"I know."

"But that's not fair! Dad didn't even say goodbye to me, and he never even came up to the nursery to see my baby. Why wouldn't he at least come up and see him? And Uncle Martin ... if he's going to try to ruin Jeremy's whole future, the least he could do was come up and meet him!"

"Felicia, try not to mind so much. They were going to say goodbye to you, but you were asleep and they didn't want to bother you — "

"No that's not the reason! My dad just didn't want to bother with me. I know. He hated having me in his way. Don't think I don't know. And Uncle Martin ... why should he care?" Felicia turned and slowly carried her child back upstairs.

THE CITY TRAFFIC had thinned when Martin drove down into the basement parking area of his apartment house. He was delighted to be home. The past week had been a strain of the kind he didn't like. There had been no real closeness between him and Mildred, but he at least had known she was there. Now, coming back to New York, he still thought of her as being "there, at Tanglewood."

He rode upstairs in the silent, plush elevator, all the way to the top where his penthouse gave him total privacy. The woman who came in during the day was always gone when he got home at night. Now, at two-fifteen in the morning, he was alone even in the hallway outside his apartment.

Inside his apartment he turned on a hall light that spread dimly into the living room, the den, the library and the master bedroom. As he walked toward his bedroom he began removing his clothes. He dropped his coat over a chair, loosened his tie and left it on a table and began unbuttoning his shirt. It had been a long drive.

On the threshold of his bedroom Martin looked up from his shirt front, his eyes drawn by the eyes that stared at him, and with a jolt of profound shock saw a baby sitting in the center of the room; just sitting, staring, small legs bent, tiny plump hands on dimpled knees. The snaps on his diaper cover gleamed in the soft light from the hall, even though he sat in shadows. There seemed to be a kind of glow emanating from him so that he was almost amorphous, a small figure bathed in source-less light.

*Where the hell did you come from?*

*Who brought you here?*

*Who the hell is playing games — !*

The smile began on the baby's face, spreading, a rounding O that showed pink gums, pink tongue, no hint of teeth, an unholy glee, spreading, spreading until Martin felt himself respond and begin returning the little fellow's grin. The hands lifted toward him, slowly, appealingly.

He was pretty damned cute.

Martin bent forward to pick him up.

WHEN THE CALL came from New York, Celta thought with a terrible sinking of her heart that Martin had already made the arrangements for Felicia and Jeremy. The voice identified himself as Turner Charleston, Martin Marchant's attorney. She replied with a polite, "Yes, sir?"

"To whom am I speaking, please?"

"Celta, an employee of the late Mrs. Stewart."

"Celta, I'm afraid I have shocking, bad news. You will need to relate it as best you can to the relatives there of Mr. Marchant. He was murdered last night."

Celta reached for a kitchen chair and dragged it near the wall phone and sat down, her knees almost buckling from beneath her before she was settled.

The voice over the phone said, "I say there, Celta, did you hear me?"

"Yes sir."

"Are you all right?"

"Yes, I'm all right now. You said he was murdered?"

"Yes. His partner called, and asked me to tell the relatives down there. I understand there are only a couple of children? So they probably will not come for the funeral?"

"No. Probably not. Did he ... was it a mugging? Someone on the street?"

"No, whoever it was had gotten into his apartment. He was found in his bedroom. The police aren't sure yet if there was also a robbery, but it doesn't seem as though there was. If you have any questions, you can call me at this number — do you have a pad and pencil?"

"Yes."

Celta wrote down the name and number in a spidery scrawl. After the phone call ended she sat in silence, numb, blank. A maid came out of the utility room and went toward the back stairway. She was carrying at least a dozen neatly folded diapers.

At the other end of the kitchen the other maid dropped something into the sink with a clatter and a soft exclamation of disgust. And Celta's mind clicked into action.

*Now there won't be any arrangements made for either Felicia or Jeremy.* Martin had been killed before he could do anything about their future.

Questions that she hadn't asked crowded into her mind. She checked the number carefully, and dialed. A secretary put her through to Turner Charleston.

"There are some things I have to ask you, Mr. Charleston, but I was so stunned by your call that I just couldn't think. I hope I'm not interrupting anything important."

"Nothing that can't wait, Miss ..."

"I want to know how he was killed. Was he shot?" It was asked in an almost buried hope. For Felicia's sake. Yes, even for the sake of the bairn.

"No, he wasn't, Celta. It appeared to be knifings, although that report was not definite. It was a brutal attack, without a doubt. That's about all I can tell you at this time. After the pathologist is finished I might have more information."

"Was the attack mostly to his face?"

A slight hesitation, a wondering; Celta could almost see the man behind his desk pause and frown at her questions. "Uh ... yes."

"What about his eyes, Mr. Charleston?"

The man's voice was suddenly sharp. "Why are you asking these questions?"

She spoke the first thing that entered her mind, that was, in a way, true. "I had a vision, Mr. Charleston, that's all. And I just wondered how he had died."

"A vision." His voice had softened, grown suddenly friendly. He sounded as though he were smiling. "My late wife had visions occasionally. She convinced me that some people actually are psychic."

"Then ... his eyes?"

The man cleared his throat softly, became deadly serious. "Yes. The attack seemed to be viciously concentrated on the eyes and throat. It was a sight I hope never to see again. I have no idea who could have done this. The police wonder if he might have picked up a hitchhiker and taken him home with him. But they have no leads that I've heard of. Your vision seems to have been accurate about the death. Do you have any ideas on who might have done it, or why?"

"No," Celta said quickly. "No ideas. And I hope you will keep my telling you of this in confidence, Mr. Charleston. I know nothing about Mr. Marchant's life, or death."

What good would it to do tell him anything? He would never believe. They would call her insane and put her away somewhere, and the bairn would be left free. Free? How could he be fettered?

Celta went into her old rooms off the kitchen, a tiny apartment of sitting room and bedroom and private bath, and bent to her knees by the side of her bed and lay her head on her arms as she hadn't done since she was a girl at her old home in Ireland. And she prayed the best she could, but there seemed no answers available. Yet in her need an answer came: *guardian*. A single word, no more, but spoken as clearly into her mind as though from beyond. She got up from her knees, and wondered at this answer. Guardian? Guard Felicia? Protect her?

*Guard Jeremy.*

Stay near him, sit with him through the nights if possible, try to find a way to stop him. Become Jeremy's guardian, and thereby protect the world. It was up to her to keep Jeremy here, to make sure he wasn't taken away. But she had to make one try at convincing Felicia she should leave, go to her father, go to school. *Anywhere.* Forget she ever had a child.

She went upstairs with renewed vigor and spirit.

Felicia, dressed in blue cashmere sweater and denim jeans, sat on the floor in front of the baby. Between them were scattered toys, rubber blocks that Celta recognized as having originally belonged to Mildred, and other, newer plastic animal figures. The baby's face was alert, fascinated by the game Felicia was creating for him. They were happy, delighting in the presence of each other. Felicia looked up at Celta and smiled.

"He loves to knock the blocks over. Isn't that great? I tell him to wait until I have them all stacked, and then I tell him to go ahead, and he does. Like this. Okay, Jeremy, knock 'em down."

Jeremy's hand swept out, and the stack of blocks tumbled soundlessly in all directions. He laughed, Felicia laughed, but Celta could not even bring herself to smile. Felicia looked up again for her approval; when she saw none, disappointment crossed her face taking the laughter away.

Celta said, "Something has happened, Felicia."

"What?"

Celta looked at Jeremy, bright eyes gleaming over the fist he had raised to his mouth. He was making baby noises around the hand.

"Put him in his crib and come with me."

Felicia obeyed without question, and followed Celta into the nurse's bedroom next to the nursery. Celta closed the door.

"Your Uncle Martin is dead. He was killed the night he went back to New York, Felicia. They called just a few minutes ago."

Felicia's mouth had opened, lips parting slightly. Uncle Martin was almost a stranger to her, and his death, although unexpected, did not touch her. She said, "Am I supposed to go up there for the funeral, or are they bringing his body down here to the family crypt?"

"No, his body isn't being brought down here. I think his partner is taking care of the burial. And you aren't expected to go up if you don't want to. Felicia, please sit down and listen. I've got something to tell you, and I don't know how to tell it so you'll understand how serious it is."

Felicia's eyes did not leave Celta as she obeyed her. The way she gazed up at Celta was unnerving, her deep blue eyes so trusting, so waiting and curious. At that moment Celta wanted to keep silent, rather than hurt this girl — child — who had been hurt too much. But Felicia's own life was possibly dependent on making her believe what Celta felt was the truth.

While Celta delayed, composing her words mentally, Felicia asked, "Does Dad know? Did anyone call him?" But then answered it herself. "I don't suppose there's any hurry about it. He's just got back; he won't be wanting to come back for Uncle Martin's funeral. They hardly knew each other. I don't think Dad every liked Uncle Martin very well, do you? He might have been envious of Uncle Martin, for Dad was not that rich. His travel agency is doing okay, though, I guess. He spent a lot of time with it. He was hardly ever home when I lived with him. But that was okay. I didn't have anything to say to him anyway. Well, Celta, what is it? I need to get back to Jeremy. He was having so much fun with the blocks and the little animals. I was telling him the names of those little plastic prehistoric animals before you came in and he was trying to repeat their names after me. Can you imagine him saying tyrannosaurus? His little mouth was twisting in all directions, and he looked so serious! *I* think that instead of being subnormal and retarded, he's a genius! That's what I think."

"A genius? I don't know what geniuses are. I never saw one. I want you to listen to me, Felicia. Nobody has told you about how your mother was killed —"

"An animal ... ?"

"Do you really believe there is an animal in our own woodland that is big enough to kill any human? Or vicious enough to kill like that?"

Felicia said slowly, "No." And then, with rising inflection in her voice, "What do you mean, Celta? Was she murdered?"

"Yes, I think so. By the same creature who murdered your uncle Martin, Felicia, because their deaths are alike from what I heard. Their heads were mutilated, and the — uh — the eyes torn out." It had been difficult for Celta to say, and more difficult to watch the flash of pain in Felicia's face.

"Who would do that?" the girl whispered. "*Why*?"

"I think that bairn in there did that," Celta said with sudden passion, pointing her entire arm. "He's not what you think he is, my child. He's a monster in the form of a baby. Now he is killing off the entire family, and if you don't get away, and stay away, he's going to kill you, too, someday."

Celta paused for breath, but Felicia said nothing. She stared incredulously at the elderly woman who stood a few feet away, body tensed almost to breaking, whispering these terrible accusations.

"Your mother wouldn't listen to me," Celta went on more slowly. "I warned her right at the start. She called it old-world superstition. But I know that all the old so-called superstition is based on fact. They call this kind of bairn a changeling. That means the dark spirits, the evil spirits that are part of the darkness that never ends, comes out and goes into the bodies of infants who are dying anyway. Or maybe they kill them, I don't know. Or maybe ..." She stopped, and looked at Felicia, a sudden speculation in her eyes. Felicia was chilled by Celta's words, chilled deeply, as deeply as that night on the hill, when they kept rising, swaying, all of them the image of the other, so alike so huge, but seeming to change before her very eyes.

Celta had resumed talking: "But they can't be normal bairns, you see. They can't laugh, and they can't cry. And usually they never talk or make a sound. That bairn in there, he makes noises, I know, and he laughs, but he don't ever cry, and he never will. And in the still hours of the night he goes into a kind of trance and that is when these things happen. He can leave his body and go right out through the walls — "

Felicia stood up, face white. "No!" she screamed, and the single word came back to them faintly in echo from the cavernous house. "You are insane! He didn't ... he can't ..."

Celta reached out for her, fearing what she had done, wishing she could take back those words. Felicia looked as though she would faint. She turned her back toward Celta and held onto the chair she had been sitting in.

The girl cried, "Don't touch me! Leave me alone."

Celta stood waiting, one hand to her mouth. When Felicia spoke again her voice was softer and far calmer. And there was a decisiveness in it that chilled Celta.

"I want you to leave, Celta. I will have Clint take you wherever you want to go, but I want you out of this house before nightfall, is that clear? And furthermore, if you call my father about this incredible nonsense, I will — I will have you committed to an insane asylum for the rest of your life. If you call my father at all with any of these cruel lies of yours, I will have you committed. I mean it, Celta. I think I could, since you have no family here in the States. Now please go." Felicia turned to face Celta, her body straight and tall. "I want you never again to go near my baby, is that clear, Celta?"

Celta nodded. She was crushed, yet not really surprised. Had she actually thought the *mother* of the bairn would listen if the grandmother wouldn't? Felicia saw him only as he wished to be seen, charming, sweet, a baby boy who had only to reach out his hand and she would go to him.

Mildred had responded one time too often.

And Felicia? When was her time coming?

Celta went downstairs to her private rooms, those rooms she had lived in during most of her years at Tanglewood. She had moved a few of her clothes upstairs to the nurse's bedroom, but all her other things were downstairs. She had an album of photographs from the early years here. In one picture Mildred, a small girl in a frilly white dress, stood holding her hand before going to church. In another, Mildred sat in the rocking chair in the nursery, holding Felicia fifteen years ago, when the baby was only a couple of weeks old. These were precious to Celta, for the Marchants had become her loved ones. In Ireland were the graves of parents who were far away in her past. In Ireland, too, were cousins and childhood friends, but she had hardly communicated with them in the past twenty years. They had families and interests that did not include her, an old maid who had gone to America, dimly remembered.

Celta had no luggage. She had never had need for any. In years past the grandmother Marchant had tried to give her vacations, but there was no place Celta wanted to go. So she had burrowed in at Tanglewood, becoming a part of the family. And now she was being sent away, and there was nothing to pack her belongings in.

She began bringing dresses out from the closet, folding them, laying them neatly on her bed. She would have to go upstairs for the others later. Her hands trembled as she worked. She wondered at times about her sanity. Perhaps both Mildred and Felicia were right, and she needed to be put away. Perhaps the call from the lawyer in New York had been just another of her fantasies.

*His head had turned slowly, and he had looked at her, and he had known that she knew ... and his eyes had not been human, nor animal, but something far less ... or far more.*

FELICIA STAYED for a while in the bedroom after Celta had gone so quietly, so beaten, with shoulders slumped and feet dragging. *How had she dared*? The anger Felicia felt weakened her, and mingled with the memory she refused to acknowledge, the deep-seated fear, that she had tried to ignore, to push to the recesses of her being where it belonged. She who slept with her lights on could not face what Celta charged. There was some kind of terrible conspiracy against her, and against her baby ... just because he was different.

It wasn't true. What Celta said ... what she implied ... Jeremy could not, would not ... *it wasn't true.*

From the nursery came a call that sounded to Felicia like, "Mama?" It was the same voice, the same calling she heard during the quiet hours of the night, outside her brightly lighted bedroom, in the hallway. *Mama ... Mama ...* And it woke her no sooner than she slept, so that she had found it easier to spend the greater part of each night in the nursery with him. But how had Celta dared suggest that he, her baby son, could ... would ... kill, destroy her mother, her uncle ...?

She said aloud, "I'm coming, darling."

Jeremy was standing at the side of his crib, his hands gripping the top rail and straining his body upward. He stood on his tiptoes, though short and plump yet. Seeing him, Felicia giggled. He turned loose of the top rail and reached both arms up for her, but lost his balance and sat back abruptly and with a jolt onto a large teddy bear. He looked so surprised that Felicia laughed outright.

"You little silly," she said, and knelt beside the crib and pushed her face between two of the white wood bars. The disappointed droop of his mouth curved into a smile of glee as he reached for her, his fingers coming through the bars to her face and clutching her cheeks.

"Not so hard, Jeremy!" she said with difficulty as his fingers pinched her cheeks. The pain was increasing as his smile widened and the tips of his fingers dug into her skin. She gripped his wrist in her hands and forced them away from her face. She was no longer indulgent when she said fiercely, "I said not so hard, Jeremy, and I meant it!" But when he laughed aloud she relented. After all, it was only a game to him, she saw, and he did not understand.

As she held his wrists it occurred to her that he hadn't eaten lately, and she released him. She fixed a bottle and placed it in his hands. He looked at her quizzically for a moment, for hadn't she always held him and given him the bottle against her breast? But she stood silent and removed from him, looking down at him, and after a moment he flopped backwards onto the teddy bear and, holding the bottle with both hands, began working on it. His eyes closed in ecstasy.

Felicia moved away from the crib and started cleaning up the room, those chores she had always left for Celta. She put away baby clothes she hadn't used, folded diapers that had become unfolded as she grabbed two instead of one. She was remembering ... Celta holding her when she fell and cut her knees ... Celta rocking her. A first memory, not of her mother or her father, but of Celta, reading to her from one of the little picture books, so tattered now. Lovely little stories that excited and charmed. Celta's voice, Celta's laughter. And problems that could always be taken to Celta. Where had she gone when she first became afraid that something was wrong with her, that her nightmare experience in the woods was not over? Not to her mother, but to Celta.

*I haven't had my periods, Celta ... I'm afraid ... I don't feel good ... I don't feel like going to school. My stomach feels funny.*

She saw that Jeremy had gone to sleep with the bottle of milk in his mouth. Milk had run out of one corner of his mouth and down onto his chin, but he didn't feel it. His mouth drooped moistly around the reddish-brown nipple.

Felicia took the bottle, pulled a blanket over him, stood for a moment looking down at him. Then she left the nursery and went downstairs to Celta's rooms.

A few small piles of clothing lay on Celta's bed, and between them the beginning pile of mementoes. Felicia recognized a small ivory elephant she had given Celta for Christmas a long time ago. Her mother had taken her shopping and Felicia, five or six years old, had fallen in love with the elephant. Felicia remembered clinging to it adamantly. It was for Celta. Celta would love it, too. Felicia had forgotten it existed.

Celta was at her chest of drawers, peering in, undecided about what to remove and what to leave. She looked up when Felicia came across the threshold.

Felicia said, "I'll help you put your things away again, Celta. I came down to say I don't really want you to go. I want you to stay here as long as you want to, but I have to tell you not to come up to the nursery any more, so perhaps you won't want to stay. I mean, I have to run my own business now, and my son's. I don't want you to call my dad, or anyone! I want you to move down here, and stay down here. I'm going to be moving into the nursery bedroom, so I'd like you to send up someone to help carry my things. Will you stay, Celta?"

Celta looked at the girl, so lovely in her youth, and wanted to take her into her arms and hold her for a moment. She didn't move, except to close the drawer.

"I don't need help to put my things away."

"You will stay, then?"

Celta nodded. "Of course I'll stay."

Felicia ran to her and threw her arms around Celta's bony shoulders, and for a short while they hugged.

"Oh Celta, I'm so glad. I'm sorry I said so many hateful things. I don't ever want you to leave, ever! You're like my very own grandma."

"I'm sorry too, dear, that I said anything." They drew apart, and Celta raised a roughened hand and touched the smooth face of the girl. Felicia saw in her eyes the concern, the worry, but she turned her mind away from the image of torn and bloody flesh, the image of death she saw in Celta's eyes.

# CHAPTER 15

Celta sat in her room, rocking, and embroidered one of the picture kits that she had collected from Christmases and birthdays past. It was the first time she had opened any of them. This one was a bucolic scene of a country home with trees and flowers and of a blue pond on which mallard and Peking ducks floated tranquilly. The house had a thatched roof, and red roses wound up a trellis by the door. All colors of flowers lined the flagstone walk, and on the threshold stood a little girl wearing a dress that came to her ankles and a bonnet pushed back on yellow curls. The kit had been a gift from Felicia, either for birthday or Christmas, Celta couldn't remember which. She could remember the conversation though: "I'll work on it when I retire, and frame it and hang it on my wall, and perhaps I'll live in a place just like that."

It seemed very quiet in these rooms today after all the upset of the morning. Imogene and the other maid had gone upstairs to help Felicia bring her clothes from the bedroom to the nursery bedroom; they had brought down Celta's few things earlier. Celta tried not to think about it. She was waiting, passing the time the best she could. Her small portable television was portraying a slow-moving soap opera that Celta listened to sporadically, without interest. It was company, that was all. She embroidered, and longed in the depths of her heart for the kind of peace that lay in the scene stamped on the linen.

When evening came she ate alone. The maids left, both going to homes in town, and darkness and silence settled. Celta waited.

At midnight she turned off the television. She was wearing a robe now, and had braided her hair freshly for the night. With close-fitting, felt house slippers soundless even on the tiled floors of the kitchen and back hall, she went up the service stairs to the second floor and into the carpeted front section of the house. The wide hall at the head of the front stairs was lighted very dimly by one wall bracket lamp. The adjacent halls were dark.

Celta went soundlessly along the hall, past the door to the nursery bedroom, to the nursery door itself. It was closed but not locked. She turned the knob slowly, and pushed it open. The night light was on as usual, throwing its small pool of pale light, leaving shadows deep and soft. They were not comforting on this still night, this night in which eyes seemed to be watching her every move, seeing into her intentions as though she had shouted them and they were echoing back at her from hall to hall to shadowed nursery.

She paused only a moment at the door, her skin cold, and colder by the moment. Then she went purposely toward the crib.

And stared in astonishment.

The crib was empty, the baby gone. Dear God, where was he? Where was Felicia? She ran into the adjoining bedroom, the bedroom in which Felicia had moved that very day, and stopped abruptly by the bed. Another soft night light on the dresser played fingers of light and shadow across the postered bed and the faces of the children, lying side by side, cheek to cheek. The baby was there in her arms, sleeping normally, cuddled closely and warmly to his mother.

Weak with relief, Celta sat on the closest chair. Felicia's face was lovely ... perhaps even more so in sleep, relaxed as it was and free from worry. And the bairn! No picture in the world ever gave out more innocence than that one.

Celta sat for several minutes watching them. Sometimes the baby's mouth moved, suckling in his dreams, and his eyelids twitched. Sometimes he moved slightly, wriggling beside Felicia as he had wriggled in her womb. Her arms continued to hold him, making allowances for his movements, opening slightly, closing again. His head stayed against hers, making a soft indentation in her cheek.

There was no strange spell this night, no cold lifelessness in his body, no death knell sounding in someone's life. It was as though peace had rained upon them suddenly, for a time at least, and even the shadows in the room seemed softer and less dangerous.

Celta began to feel her tiredness as though the tension and anxiety of past months had been holding her together. With one last look at the sleeping pair she went quickly out of the room and downstairs.

She stretched out on her own bed with a great sigh, and pulled up soft warm blankets against the wintery night. The room was dark and still, and at that moment of rest almost as peaceful as the scene in linen.

CELTA HAD SET a pattern that first night that continued through the next two months, those long months of winter, ice storms and snows that transformed Tanglewood into the exquisite beauty of a glittering wonderland. Every night she made her way up the stairs and into the nursery and the nursery bedroom, and every night found the same peaceful scene.

During the day Felicia brought Jeremy downstairs for longer periods, showing him almost shyly to Celta, her eyes begging in silence for Celta's approval and love.

"See how grand he looks today, Celta," Felicia would say, standing her baby on the floor, holding his hands to keep him from falling, showing him off. "Don't you think he's the prettiest baby you ever saw?"

"No prettier than his mother was."

Felicia was not comforted by remarks like that, and began urging Celta to take the child, to hold him, to love him. And, as though to see to it that it happened, began asking her to babysit.

"Would you mind keeping him, Celta, while I have Clint take me to town? I want to buy Jeremy some new clothes. Something really cute. And if you'll give me the grocery list I'll fill that, too."

It became a weekly ritual, the bringing of Jeremy into the kitchen to stay with Celta while Clint drove Felicia to town. On her return Celta helped unpack children's books, games, toys, and sometimes an excessive amount of red licorice twist candy, a favorite of Felicia's.

There was no mention of school, and no one came to the house to question why Felicia was not in school. Celta assumed the school officials of the county thought the girl was still in private school. It didn't really matter to Celta. Hadn't she herself gone only through book five? So long as a person could read and write and get a good job, what was the purpose of school? And of course in Felicia's circumstances, where she was provided for the rest of her life, whether or not she went to school didn't matter. Celta said nothing. She had received her orders; she would stand by them. So long as nothing bad happened.

And so far, all was good. When Felicia left Jeremy with her, he behaved just like any eight-month-old baby. Celta put him on the floor at her feet, gave him balls of rolled knitting yam to play with, and continued with her needlework. Jeremy kept busy with yarn, unrolling it, turning away only when he heard the back door open, bringing his mother home. Then he would start laughing softly, go onto his hands and knees and take off across the polished tiled floor of the kitchen, only to sit back and raise his arms eagerly toward her, whimpering, a sound that was almost a sob, almost laughter. Felicia always put down her bundles there and caught him up into her arms. Clint, behind her with the grocery bags, grinned at them as though they were the sun just broken through the clouds.

At Christmas there was a huge cedar tree from the meadow. Clint helped Felicia to decorate it, and there were more packages than Celta had ever seen under any tree before in her life. From Felicia's father came a card, a brief note, and a bracelet of exotic stones collected somewhere on his travels. For Jeremy, nothing. When Felicia saw that Jeremy had been forgotten, or ignored, she quietly put both her present and the Christmas card aside, and Celta knew she would never touch them again. Eventually, Celta tucked them into a drawer in the hall table.

Every day Celta wondered how long this peace would last. And every day, every night, seemed an accomplishment. Every time she saw Felicia again, saw that she was well, she knew solace.

Jeremy was nine months' old, a picture of physical beauty and good health, husky, strong, with ready laughter and bright eyes, the day the doorbell rang. He had begun taking steps without aid, going from one chair or table to another and thereby working his way about in any room, or out of it if the door was open. If thwarted in his advance on his feet, he dropped quickly to his knees and hands and raced on. Celta found him harder and harder to keep up with on the afternoons he was in her charge.

Both Jeremy and Felicia had gone upstairs for their afternoon naps on that warm February day that the musical chimes of the front doorbell sounded in the foyer and kitchen. Startled, Celta dropped her needlework, and the maid at the sink jumped and squealed softly, and then laughed at herself.

"Golly!" Imogene said as she wiped her hands on her tiny white apron. She had been preparing the dinner salad — spinach and cauliflower and green onions, as well as hardboiled eggs. "It's been so long since I heard that sound that it about scared the britches off me!"

Celta said, "It's probably a salesman brought out by the warm weather. I'll go, Imogene."

"Are you sure?" the younger woman asked, as though Celta were scarcely able to make the walk to the front door.

"Yes, I'll go."

And a short time later Celta opened the door. A tall young boy stood on the step; behind him, on the winter-dried grass of the lawn, a bicycle was lying on its side. The boy's good-looking face flushed slightly as he looked at Celta and smiled.

"Is Felicia home?"

"Felicia?" Celta stared at him. She vaguely remembered this face, the copper red hair glistening in the sun, the soft brown eyes and curling lashes, the full mouth. But now a furriness was added to the cheeks and chin, the beginnings of a golden-red beard. A boy she had once looked down to, now looked down to her.

"Yes, ma'am," the boy said, looking uncomfortable.

"She's home," Celta said quickly. "Just come on in, and I'll go up and get her. I think she's taking a nap."

"I can come back some other time — "

"No, she'd be disappointed. I'll just be a minute."

"Thanks. I'll wait out here. The weather's nice. I thought she might like to go bike riding with me, if she was home."

Celta left the door open in case he should change his mind and decide to come on into the house to wait. This, she thought as she hurried up the stairs, would do Felicia good.

Felicia and Jeremy lay on the new fur rug in the nursery, one of the additions Felicia had recently made. But neither was asleep. Felicia was reading from one of the small picture books, and Jeremy lay drowsily at her side, his head on her arm. Both of them looked up curiously as Celta came into the room. Felicia's hand, with the book, dropped limply to her side; her only movement.

"You've got company," Celta said, feeling the unusual pull of a smile at her lips.

"Company!" Felicia sat up, easing Jeremy's head off her arm. "Who?"

"I don't remember his name, but he used to come out here quite a bit. He's the boy with the red hair."

"Not Gary Appleby!"

"Yes, that's the one. I'd forgot his name."

"He's the boy who used to write me notes in school. Mushy ones. What did you tell him?"

"I told him you'd be right down. He wants you to go for a bicycle ride."

"Oh but I can't."

"And why can't you?"

"What about Jeremy?"

"I can stay with Jeremy. He was about to go to sleep anyway, wasn't he?"

"But he's awake now."

"He'll go back to sleep. Put him in his crib and give him a bottle, and I'll sit with him. He'll be all right. You need to get out and be with someone your own age."

Felicia's face became animated, excitement tightening her eyes. She got to her feet. "I would kind of like to see someone from my old school, hear the gossip and everything. Gary will know what's going on, and he'll tell me. He's not one of those big silent types. He's kind of girlish and scrawny and talkative. A born salesman, somebody said."

"Not anymore," Celta said, as she reached out for Jeremy. After all, she could settle him for the afternoon. "He's grown up. Even got himself a beard of sorts. He was about ready to run, too, so you'd better hurry before he does." Felicia pulled her sweater down over the top of her jeans and hurried into the bedroom to brush her hair, and for a moment it seemed she had forgotten the baby boy who was sitting on the rug, his head turned after her, ignoring the hands that reached down for him.

Celta bent lower and picked him up, groaning faintly under his weight. He was at least twenty-five pounds now, a chunky, plump bairn, and hard for an old woman to pick up from the floor. However, she only only Felicia to go on and, for this afternoon, be the girl she deserved to be.

A moment later Felicia came back into the nursery, her hair smoothly and freshly brushed. She put her arms happily around both Celta and Jeremy, hugged them, kissed them both. "I'll be back!" she said, and was gone.

The baby was heavy in Celta's arms, and quiet. But now that Felicia was gone from the room, her footsteps fading away down the hallways, he began to whimper, to push against Celta and lean in the direction Felicia had gone.

"No!" Celta said. "Let her out of your sight for a change. She's been with you night and day ever since ..." *your grandmother was killed.* This, she couldn't say aloud. She put the baby down into the crib where he instantly pulled himself up, strained upward as though to climb out over the side. He clung and whimpered, his knuckles white with the strength of his clutch on the top rail. Celta brought his bottle and handed it to him. He pushed at it angrily, his face twisting as though he would start crying. But before tears came, he sat back into the crib, pushed himself into a corner and dropped his hands between his bent legs. The bottle lay beside him, untouched. He seemed unaware that

Celta was in the room. For a long minute she stood looking down at him, but his eyes did not leave the door through which Felicia had gone.

"Why are you acting like this, Jeremy?" Celta asked. "When your mama goes to town, you don't act like this."

He seemed oblivious to her, staring past her al the door, deaf to her voice.

"Jeremy," she tried again, "would you like to go down to the kitchen with Celta and play with the basket of yarn?"

Still no response. His face was expressionless, set, waiting, and Celta began to fear that he was going into one of his spells. She reached down with her hand outstretched and moved it slowly cross his vision, close to his eyes.

"Jeremy, *Jeremy*!"

His eyes swung abruptly upward, pinpointing her, holding her, and the movement of his head was so swift that she had no warning. In the past two months he had grown four teeth, two above and two below, and suddenly these were clamped onto the side of her hand in a bite as darting and as vicious as the wildest of animals, or the most poisonous of snakes.

Celta gasped with the pain and jerked away. Four drops of blood oozed from the wounds in the fleshy edge of her palm. She hurried away, closing the door behind her as she ran into the hall. She gathered her apron up and pressed it against her hand, and then she stopped, listening, every nerve of her body alerted to the sound that came from beyond the closed door.

Hisses, as of a thousand snakes, virulent, lethal, threatening. Celta's flesh grew frigid, all blood drawn away, leaving it tightened and shriveled. For even the dark fairies of the woodlands, the changelings, those feared creatures of her youth and the old worlds had no comparison with this. Her imagination was not capable of delving into the mysteries of the creature beyond the door. At the moment all she could do was run, hurry as fast as her aging bones could carry her, and close the door to her private rooms and tremblingly try to cover her wounds ... and try to forget what she had heard.

# CHAPTER 16

"Hi," Felicia said at the front door, feeling suddenly shy. The scrawny little freckle-faced, red-haired boy who passed mushy notes to her in school had grown into a tall, handsome boy who was masculine and a bit shy himself. He looked down at her from six feet with a half-smile on his full, sensual, soft lips. But only his lips were soft now. There was nothing soft in the wide shoulders, or the strong bones of his face.

"How're you?" he asked. And then, "Gosh, you've grown up."

"You too."

"Did you get my birthday card?"

"Yes. Thanks."

They looked at each other for a few moments, quiet, embarrassed, revelations bursting like silent fireworks about them. A childhood attraction was maturing, blossoming, ripening. He saw the pink moistness of her mouth, the bulge of breasts and hips, the slim narrowness of waistline. He longed to touch her, to feel the smoothness of her skin, the round curves of her body, the silkiness of her long hair. And she wondered about the touch of his hands, their warmth, and looked at his lips and knew they would one day touch hers. Instinctively she stepped backwards one step and lowered her eyes.

"Hey," he said, "have you still got your ten speed bike?"

This was a comfortable subject, and she raised her face toward his. "I sure do, but I haven't ridden it in a long, long time. I don't know if I could anymore."

"Sure you could. Come on, let's go get it and go for a ride."

They spent the afternoon riding up and down the road in front of Tanglewood, sometimes stopping to talk, sometimes talking while they rode leisurely. And they raced, ten-speed against ten-speed, but when he drew away from her he'd turn back to let her catch up. She didn't win. She had no desire to win. It was good knowing that he was stronger and more capable than she. She liked knowing that he was taller, a bit older, protectively masculine.

"I thought you were away at school somewhere," he said, riding slowly beside her into the tunnel of tree-covered roadway. "I didn't know whether to come out or not, but since it was so nice today, I just thought I would."

"I'm glad you did, Gary. I was away at school but after my mother died I came home."

"You mean you're not going to school at all?"

"No."

"But why? I mean, don't you even want to?"

"I don't know." She didn't meet his eyes. She hadn't even thought about school in these past months. She had thought only of being with her baby, but that was something she knew she didn't want to tell Gary. "Maybe I'll come back," she said, hoping to put an end to that subject.

"Hey, do you remember Mary Beth?"

"Yeah! Sure."

"Well, she ran away from home, and got picked up somewhere up north and put in a school of some kind that she can't run away from, Harry said. Some of the kids think it's a reform school, but I don't know."

"What happened to her? I mean, why did she run away?"

Gary shrugged. "Who knows? I've thought about running away a few times myself, haven't you?"

Felicia giggled. "I guess so."

"Of course I won't. What I want to do is get good enough grades to get into a good college. I want to be an engineer and build things, you know, like bridges."

"Sounds interesting."

"Yeah, sure is. What about you?"

"Me? I don't know. I hadn't thought much about it."

They rode on toward Jonesboro, along the curving drive over which the treetops created a roof against the sky. On their right the cliffs fell straight down to the river, far below. They had ridden perhaps a mile when Felicia noticed the darkness falling, so quickly, as though a blanket had been thrown over the trees.

"It's getting late, Gary, I have to go back."

They stopped in the road and looked back. A covering of clouds had hastened the sunset, and the tunnel behind them was lost in shadows. Felicia felt a stirring of fear, of dread. She longed to ride swiftly through the dark route home.

"I'll go back with you," Gary said, turning his bike in the road.

"Oh no, you don't have to do that," Felicia said, half hopefully, reassured by his presence. "It's only another mile on to Jonesboro; if you came back with me you'd get caught in the dark for sure."

"No, I won't. And even if I did, so what? I know the way. I'm taking you home."

"Then let's ride as fast as we can," Felicia said. "Just don't run off and leave me."

When they came out of the trees and approached the driveway up to the house, Felicia paused, looking back into the darkened woods from which they had emerged. Gary stopped also, feet resting on the pavement.

"Is something wrong?" he asked.

She discarded her first thought, of asking him in for hot chocolate. Celta might have taken Jeremy downstairs to the kitchen. And if he went all the way to the house with her, wouldn't he expect to come in as he used to when they were younger? They had always ended their bike rides, or their swims in the river, with a snack in the kitchen. And if Jeremy was sitting there at Celta's feet, what would she say? *This is my little brother* ... No, she couldn't say that, even though everyone except her father and Celta thought it was true.

"I can go on alone from here, Gary," she said. 'Thanks a lot for riding back with me."

"Okay. Is it all right if I come out again?"

Her mood lightened. "Oh, sure. Whenever you want."

"Tomorrow? Tomorrow's Sunday, and I don't have anything I'd rather do."

"Sure, Gary. I'd like that."

He smiled at her, turned the bike and rode swiftly into the dark tunnel of trees.

Felicia watched until he was gone, then she slowly moved on toward the driveway. A sliver of sun peeked once from between the layer of clouds and the horizon, and was gone, and darkness came down heavily then. The lights in the house were coming on, in the ground floor family room at the back, and the kitchen area. The automatic yard light was shining between the barns and garages when Felicia put her bike away. The air was still mild, with only touches of coldness moving out from the forest as the shadows increased. Felicia did not hurry. It had been a great afternoon. She hadn't realized before how she had missed kids her own age, especially friendly kids. She thought about returning to school after summer vacation, and catching up meantime with her old class. Private tutoring would do it.

She entered the house at the rear, going into the service hall and from there to the brightly lighted kitchen. The woman who took care of the cleaning and the laundry was putting her coat on, preparing to leave. Imogene was still in the kitchen; dinner was almost ready.

Felicia spoke to both of them and went on looking for Celta. She was in her room, sitting by her lamp, working on embroidery. The small portable television was on, softly, but Celta was not watching. Jeremy was not there.

Felicia dropped to her knees beside Celta's chair and tipped the embroidered scene in linen down so she could see. "Beautiful," she said. "Almost finished with it, aren't you?"

"Yes. I'm going to frame it."

Celta spread it out, smoothed it, held it up for Felicia to admire.

Many fine, tedious stitches had gone into the work, and when Celta paused to look at it she felt like an artist.

"What happened to your hand?" Felicia asked. Celta dropped the hand quickly. She had bandaged it with overlapping Band-Aids, and although they hid the small wounds, there was still pain and stinging and, worse, fear and confusion again that had almost been laid to rest in these past few months.

Celta said shortly, "Jabbed it with my scissors. How was your ride?"

"Just great! I'm really glad he came out. And he's coming back tomorrow."

Felicia leaned against Celta's knee, her face glowing with a combination of the cool evening air and the excitement and anticipation Gary had brought to her. The glow warmed Celta's heart.

"I'm thinking about going back to school Celta," Felicia said. "I could start again after summer vacation, and be with my old class if I study between now and then, couldn't I?"

"Of course you could."

"I could hire a tutor, don't you think, Celta?" Her voice was lifting in enthusiasm, eager, outgoing as Celta hadn't heard since the girl was in junior high. "Don't you think I have enough allowance for that?"

"I should certainly think so."

"Then that's what I'll do. She paused. "But of course I'll have to wait until Monday. Tomorrow Gary and I might pack a picnic lunch, if the weather is still as warm as today, and ride down to Bee Bluffs. We haven't been there since we were kids."

Celta smiled. *Kids*. She said, "That would be a good place to have a picnic. Just don't get too close to the edge."

"Would you take care of Jeremy, Celta?"

Celta licked her drying lips. The pain in her hand seemed to increase with fiery pangs, throbbing, swelling, bursting at the Band-Aids. She said, "We'll see after the bairn. Just you go ahead and have a good time."

"Where is he now?" Felicia asked. "Is he still having his nap?"

Celta had trouble finding an appropriate answer. She had walked hurriedly out of the nursery and, holding her apron to her hand, come on downstairs to her private rooms, her private bath. Neither of the maids had seen her. And when the hand was bathed and bandaged she had sat down, and here she still sat, working furiously at the linen scene, trying not to think, finding it impossible to think rationally. She was reacting, that was all. She had left the child untended. For the first time in his life he had spent the greater part of the afternoon alone. There had been no call, no cry, from the nursery. Only silence. But she hadn't expected to hear a cry.

She said, "I expect he is." But then, her conscience pricking, she added, "I left him in his crib with a bottle of milk beside him."

Felicia was silent a moment longer, remaining at Celta's knee, but the glow had gone from her face. She got to her feet.

"I'll go see about him. I'll bring him down to eat with us."

When Felicia passed through the kitchen, the maid with the coat on was talking with Imogene, a last minute discussion of something that did not interest or concern Felicia. She only glanced at them and went through the swinging doors into the main hall toward the front of the house. The hall lights had been turned on, and one dim upstairs hall light had come on automatically.

But the nursery was dark. No one had come upstairs to turn on the light, nor to check on Jeremy, and when Felicia saw the darkness in the nursery, when she noted the intense quiet, the feeling of emptiness, of vacancy, panic began building. Where was her baby? Why was the room so quiet, so dark?

She felt for a light switch and flipped it, bringing the bright ceiling light on. She ran to the crib.

And she stared down upon his limp body, frozen for a moment of eternal fear, the fear that every mother dreads, held immobile for that moment. He lay on his back, his arms and legs thrown limply out, sprawled unnaturally. His mouth was slightly open, his eyes glazed and blank.

Then she screamed and screamed, and ran, out into the hall and down the stairs, her cries echoing in the large house. As the screams reached the kitchen and Celta's rooms, Felicia's voice began forming a word, "*Celta! Celta!*"

They hurried to meet her, colliding together as they came to the swinging doors, both maids and Celta. Felicia flung herself at the elderly woman.

"Jeremy!" Felicia cried, "something's wrong with Jeremy!"

Celta took the lead, hurrying on past Felicia in silence, her face drained of all color. The two maids gave each other looks of questioning dread, and followed behind Celta and Felicia. At the nursery they stood back out of the way, just outside the door, and peered in silently.

Celta looked in upon Jeremy, a quick glance. The face she turned toward the women in the hall was gray, lips colorless. She saw the door was open, and she went to it, and in the process of closing it she said to the two maids, "There's nothing you can do, just go on back downstairs." She closed the door in their faces. Her thoughts whipped through their possible reactions. They would gossip, they would wonder, they would question her own actions. It couldn't be helped. Felicia was hanging over the crib half screaming and half crying, and Celta hurried back to stand beside her. She reached down for the baby and shook him, with no results. His body remained as limp, as seemingly lifeless, as a rag doll. She rushed to the basin in the bathroom and brought back a washcloth dripping with cold water and bathed his face. Still he lay, gazing blindly up at the ceiling, water dripping from his face, plastering his hair to the pale forehead.

"Oh Lord," Celta said, her mind suddenly spinning into action. The boy who had spent the afternoon with Felicia was riding through the dark toward Jonesboro. He was probably halfway there, in the tunnel of overhanging trees. "Call the police, Felicia!"

Felicia was stunned into silence. Police? *Police*? An ambulance? "*Is he dying, Celta*?"

"No! It's a spell that he has sometimes. He's not dying. I'll call. I'll make the call."

She started toward the hallway and the phone in the library, but remembered the women. Even if they had obeyed her command and gone downstairs, they would still be watching and waiting. For the first time since Mildred's death, she went into those rooms, leaving doors behind her standing open. On the desk was a private phone that had no extensions in the house. It took long moments of anxious fumbling with the phone book in the drawer to find the number of Jonesboro police.

When she received an answer she said, "There's been an accident on Tanglewood road out of Jonesboro. Will you hurry, please?"

The man who had taken the call asked calmly, "What kind of accident, Miss — ?"

Without answering, Celta hung up the phone, then she turned, she saw Felicia standing white-faced in the doorway, staring at her, eyes wide, accusing. Felicia began shaking her head, and her voice trembled.

"Aren't you even going to call a doctor?" Felicia sked.

Celta answered, "A doctor won't do any good." She pushed past Felicia and went back into the nursery and stood looking down into the crib. What you should do now, instead of worrying about calling a doctor, is get down on your knees and pray to the Lord to take that boy safely home!"

GARY RODE leisurely through the dark, the small headlight on his bike sweeping before him, opening up a pathway down the center of the road. The air had turned frosty, coming through his sweater and raising goosebumps, so that sometimes he stood up on his bike pedals and pumped hard just to warm up. Comfortable again, he sat down and set the bike to coast around the bends in the road above the cliff.

He was nearing the end of the darkest area when he heard something that raised chills of a different kind. A cry in the forest to his left, somewhere in the rise of hills and trees, an animal cry that he did not recognize. It brought swiftly to mind the death of Felicia's mother last fall, in those very woods but closer, much closer to the house. He had been among the posse that had gone into the woods to search for the animal. He had even seen the place where she had died — the signs of struggle in the soft black soil of the forest floor, the scattered leaves, the broken twigs, the dark patches of blood here and there among them.

He stood up on his bike and began to pump hard, switching the gears to high, following the swinging and erratic tunneled light in front, seeing its inadequacy for the first time, its narrowness of illumination.

The animal cry came again, softly, like the quivering call of a screech owl, just above the bank to his left and to the front so that he abruptly hit his brakes, sliding to a stop. He licked his suddenly dried lips, and found breathing difficult as he stared into the darkness on the hillside.

Silence dropped abruptly, and Gary was frozen within it, feeling vulnerable as he never had before, knowing the light on his bicycle was now a beacon to whatever it was that stood in the darkness. In quiet desperation he jerked the front wheel of his bicycle to the left so that the light swept among the tangle of tree trunks, vines, limbs, roots on the hillside. But there was nothing, not even the reflection from the animal's eyes. The night was sadistically silent, waiting, offering him no solace whatsoever.

A long breath jumped through his chest and throat and expelled from his mouth in a hiss. He sucked it in again and held it, and straightened the front wheel, and the light swept back onto the road, and there, standing at the side of the road, a small hand gripping the end of an exposed tree root, his short little legs fat and dimpled, stood a baby boy.

Gary's breath shot out of his lungs, taking the fear along and leaving total, blank surprise. "Jesus Christ!" he said aloud. "Who left you here?"

CELTA STOOD tense at the side of the crib, praying in silence and without words for a change in the bairn, for the return, the deep sleep of exhaustion — or satisfaction? — that indicated he was once again humanly powerless. Beside her Felicia stood as though waiting for a command. And suddenly Celta's mind began working in a stumbling, erratic way.

"Take him up," she ordered, "and hold him, rock him. He's wanting you, that's what it is, I think, that makes him this way, that causes him to kill and destroy. He'll destroy us all when the time comes, but for now bring him back if you can." She placed her hand on the girl's back and shoved her even closer to the crib. "Go on, take him, rock him, hold him, talk to him. Maybe he'll come back to you."

She waited only until she saw Felicia raise the limp baby from the crib and, handling him as though he might break into uncountable pieces, go with him to the rocking chair. They were seated, Felicia cradling his head in her arm, against her breast, when Celta hurried out of the room.

As she had suspected, the maids were waiting in the downstairs hall, at the foot of the stairway. Their faces were tense and drawn, and a bit curious as well.

Celta pushed them both toward the hallway to the kitchen. She had a message for Alice, the one who was ready to go home to Jonesboro, and she barely considered the wording and the impression it would make. She had a double duty — to protect both the boy, and Felicia.

"Go on, Alice, hurry, and pick up the boy who came to see Felicia this afternoon. He'll be riding his bike, through the dark, but I want you to make him leave his bike and ride back to town with you. Don't leave him until he's at his own doorstep, do you hear me?"

Alice only nodded, Celta's anxiety drawn into herself. Buttoning her coat, she almost ran to the door and toward her car, parked down by the garages. Celta followed, and stood where she could watch as Alice drove out the driveway and speeded east toward Jonesboro.

"Oh Lord, don't let her be too late ... don't let her be too late ... "

FELICIA HELD her baby son close, one arm supporting the limp weight, her free hand kneading his wrists, patting his cheeks, trying to arouse him to consciousness. Celta had gone after a doctor, she was sure. She had only to wait, and the doctor would arrive, and while she held Jeremy she felt less as though she had lost him.

"Jeremy, please. Jeremy, speak to mama, please, Jeremy ... "

Her voice, soft, pleading, was a whisper in the still room. The bright ceiling light outlined his features, the terrible blankness of his eyes.

She lowered her face to his and kissed him, the soft cheek smooth and cool under her lips, cooler than normal. Was he dying after all?

She felt for his pulse, and after several seconds of growing panic she found it, faint but even, as though energy had been drawn away, leaving only a feeble flow through his heart.

She lifted him against her shoulder, as she had when he was still a tiny infant, and patted his back. He had grown so, was such a husky child now, that his knees folded against her, and his small feet with their bare, chubby toes lay on her thighs. She patted his back desperately, calling to him, casting a quick anxious look toward the door in search of a doctor, of Celta, of anyone.

But no one was coming into the nursery, nor, it seemed, even into the house. She was surrounded by a silence that gave her no hope.

Jeremy slid back onto her lap as her strength waned. She held him quietly then, her cheek resting on the top of his head. She rocked slowly at first, then faster and faster, and began crooning the favorite old nursery rhyme:

"WYNKEN, Blynken and Nod one night
Set sail in a wooden shoe ..."

THERE WAS MOVEMENT AGAINST HER, a drawing in of arms and legs convulsively, jerkily. He let out a long breath, then tipped his head back and gazed up into her face as she stared at him in silent thanksgiving. He smiled dreamily and reached for her face, his small palm cupping her cheek.

He turned toward her, his mouth coming to rest on the soft, round rise of her bosom. And his eyes closed.

"Jeremy, Jeremy, my baby."

She wept gently and quietly, her arms drawing him closer and closer, her cheek lowering to rest against the soft, dark curls.

He slept, exhausted, clinging to her with both his hands, his body curling round her stomach.

# CHAPTER 17

The police came at seven-thirty, driving past the front of the house and coming to a stop near the kitchen door. Celta had been watching and waiting, and opened the door before they were out of the car.

Although she had lived at Tanglewood for the past thirty-eight years, and both the men who approached her from the county sheriff's car had been born and reared locally, Celta did not know them, nor did they know her. Both men had ridden along the curving road going past Tanglewood all their lives, first in their family's car, later in the sheriff's car, and both had been interested and curious about the people who lived there, about the house itself. It was the last of the old plantation mansions in the area. Both of them had searched the hills back of Tanglewood in the days following the death of Mildred Marchant Stewart, but neither came to the house with the sheriff to question the people who had found her body.

Ralph Corey and Danny Rounds now approached Celta full of horror at the sight they had just left. The boy in the center of the road, the bicycle on its side. They were the ones who had gone out on the call, who had found him. The sheriff was still there, along with others from the Jonesboro police department. Then, from the other direction a car had skidded to a stop, and a woman had gotten out and started vomiting. From Jonesboro then had come the ambulance.

If it hadn't been for the telephone call, questioning the local people would not have been part of Corey and Rounds' job. They would only have begun what would be done later — search the woods again for the animal, the creature, that had killed and torn to pieces two people now. Some around town were already coming out toward the scene with rifles, shotguns, lanterns, muttering that it was another bigfoot, only far worse.

Before they could speak, Celta asked, "Is the boy all right?"

The men glanced at each other, and Ralph Corey took the initiative. "Are you the lady who called the police department about an accident?"

To delay the answer, Celta stepped aside. "Won't you come in?" She led the way on into the kitchen, then she faced them. She had made up her mind.

"I called," she said, "because I knew he was riding through that dark road where there are no houses, and I was worried about him. I didn't want the same thing to happen to him that happened to Mrs. Stewart. And now I want to know if you found him in time — is he safely at home? Is he all right?"

"Your name is Celta McDowell?"

"Yes, sir. The boy ...?"

"No, he's not all right, Miss McDowell, I'm sorry. Your call was answered, but it was already too late. Do you have anything else you can tell us about this?"

Celta turned away, staggered slightly so that Corey stepped quickly forward and helped her to a chair.

"He was killed?" she asked.

"Yes."

"Was it — the same thing that happened to Mildred?"

"Mildred Stewart? Yes, I'm afraid it was. Have you heard or seen any signs of the animal that did this?"

"No, nothing. Only the squirrels, and not many of them this time of year. Nothing in our woodland." Her hands brushed across her face. "Oh, Lord, if only he'd gone home before dark."

"Yes, ma'am. If you hear of anything, you'll let us know."

"Yes."

They started to leave. Rounds paused, and looked with concerned eyes at Celta. "Are you all right, ma'am? Are you alone here?"

Celta rose to her feet. She wanted them to leave, and if she had to project a strength she didn't feel, she would do so. "No, I'm not alone. Mrs. Stewart's daughter and young son are here."

"I would advise that none of you leave the house tonight, or any other night, without protection, until this animal is found and destroyed."

"No, sir."

Celta closed the door behind them, turned and saw Imogene's pale face in the doorway to the breakfast room. "You can go on home, now," Celta told her. "Whatever needs to be done with the dinner dishes I will do."

Imogene glanced toward the window over the sinks and drew back from the darkness beyond. "I've a notion to call one of my sons to come and get me. If I should have car trouble — "

Celta, on her way toward the service stairs, halted abruptly. She knew the danger was gone now, and would probably not have threatened Imogene even if it weren't. Not with him still as young as he was.

"You'll be all right," Celta said. "The police are all along the road now."

"Yes, you're probably right," Imogene said, frowning. "Well, then, goodnight, Celta."

Imogene went quickly across the lighted terrace and driveway to her car. Celta locked the door behind her, although she didn't know why, the lock would not keep the danger out, and turned once again toward the stairway. They were alone now, she and Felicia and the bairn. Half the county would be out roaming the hills this night, their feeble little flashlights searching for something that wasn't there. She murmured a short prayer for the innocent wild animals, hoping that all of them were in hiding on this chilly February night.

There had to be an answer to this, she thought as she slowly climbed the steep back stairs. There had to be a solution. She had to get Felicia far away from the bairn, convince her of the danger she was in;

and then she herself had to stand guard over the bairn and somehow contain him, overpower him. But, dear Lord of mercy, how?

She entered the nursery. Felicia was in the rocking chair, her face turned toward the unshaded window. In her arms she held the sleeping baby. He was curled around her, seeming to envelop her, one hand clutching her shoulder even in his sleep, his face pressed into her breast.

Felicia looked round as Celta closed the hall door. She smiled tremulously and whispered loudly, "He's asleep now."

Celta nodded, came to stand in front of the chair and look down at the child. His possessive attitude seemed voracious, as though he wished to consume his mother.

Felicia asked, again in a whisper, "Where are all the cars going? Was that a police car I saw?"

"Yes. Put the bairn in his crib."

"I'm afraid he'll wake up."

"No, he won't wake up. He'll sleep soundly for long hours now. Nothing will wake him that I know of." She bent and took the child out of Felicia's arms, pulling him away even though his hand continued to clutch Felicia's sweater. "Loosen his hand," she ordered tersely, and Felicia obeyed, bending the small fingers away one by one.

Celta took Jeremy to the crib and laid him in, and he curled into a fetal knot on his side, his thumb going to his mouth. Celta pulled two blankets over him.

"That spell he had, Felicia," she said gently. 'That was the kind of spell I was talking about when your Uncle Martin died. Was killed. Come over here and take a good look at this bairn."

Felicia came slowly, for Celta's voice had a sternness she had never heard before. Her attempt at correction was feeble. "Do you have to keep calling him that, Celta? It sounds so cold." She paused only briefly. "Something's wrong, isn't it?"

"Yes." Celta's eyes left the baby and rose to meet Felicia's. "He's killed again, Felicia."

The objections, the tears of protest that Celta steeled herself against, did not come.

"Gary?" Felicia asked.

Her voice had a quiet, flat quality. Her eye revealed a kind of still fear, like a cornered animal's.

"Yes. On the way home, just as I was afraid."

Felicia's lower lip trembled. She caught it hard between her teeth to still it. When she released it the marks of her teeth remained.

"What did you tell the police?" Felicia asked.

"The first time, when I called, I told there then was an accident. That's why they came on out here now. I expect they would have come to warn you anyway, about the animal they think killed this boy."

"Then you didn't ..."

"No, I didn't. Would they have believed me? No, no more than you, nor your mother, nor anyone."

Felicia moved closer to the crib, her hands on the rail, her head tilted sideways; she looked down at her child, sleeping curled beneath the blankets, long lashes casting a shadow on his cheeks. Her own lashes cast a similar shadow on her pale skin, and her bright hair fell forward over her shoulder. Celta watched her in silence.

"He's my baby, Celta," Felicia whispered. "You can't know how much I love him."

"I know you love him. That's why I want you to take a long look at him. You love what you see, and you don't believe the other. But for your own sake, and maybe even for his, you've got to leave him, Felicia. Go to your father's house and stay there, far away. I'll stay with the — with him, I give you my word. I'll take care of him."

Felicia moved away and stood with her back to Jeremy, her head lowered. Celta saw with great relief that it was not a rebellious stance. She was giving in, slowly. She was listening.

But she said, "I don't think I can, Celta. I can't go away knowing he's here, needing me."

"He doesn't need you, he needs only to be cared for, and I can do that. You have to go, Felicia. Get away. If you don't go willingly, I'll have to call your father and have him come and get you."

"No, don't tell him. I'll ... let me think about it. There has to be something we can do, Celta. What is it?"

"I don't know yet. If there is anything, I'll find it. But I want you safe."

Felicia cried out suddenly and fiercely, "I'm safe with him! Don't you see that? We belong together. I gave birth to him. He's mine, and I love him and need him as much as he does me. Why couldn't it have been something else that — that killed Mama and — why couldn't it really have been something else?"

"In a New York apartment that was locked from the inside?"

"But ...

Celta saw in Felicia's eyes hints of secrets, unexpressed fears of her own. Doubt. And again, belief. Celta felt it was time that she back away now, go down to her own quarters, and give the girl time alone with her ... *child*. It seemed true, so far, that he would not harm her. He wanted her, and only her, destroying all who threatened to come between them. And yet, he had wisely kept Celta. He knew he needed someone mature to help his mother, Celta thought.

"Where are you going?" Felicia asked.

"Downstairs. I'll be in my room if you need me." The door closed softly behind her. Alone, with no eyes to watch and criticize her movements, Felicia leaned over the crib and touched him lovingly, caressing his cheeks, pushing his hair, so fine and soft, back from his forehead. She felt that all around her was a world of madness. Only here, in the nursery, did love and sanity prevail. His little corduroy pants and knit shirt looked tight and binding around his chubby body. Hadn't Celta said nothing would wake him? Perhaps, if she worked slowly and gently, she could change him to his pajamas with the feet. The night was cold.

She took out clean, soft, blue pajamas that snapped up the front, and lay them on the counter. When she lifted the sleeping baby from the crib his body jerked again convulsively, nervously, legs and arms tightening, drawing close. But his eyes didn't open, and when she laid him on the counter to undress him, he was sleeping again. Handling him gently and slowly, she removed his outer clothes and slipped him feet first into the pajamas. Then she held him in her arms and rocked slowly and quietly by the unshaded window, staring at her reflection, at the baby in her arms. She forgot to go down for dinner. She forgot that she hadn't eaten since noon. She was existing in the moment, the warmth of the child sustaining her.

She usually took him to bed with her, where, both of them awake, they played small games like Piggy, and patty cake, until he began to yawn and finally slept. Every night had been the same, until tonight. Not thinking or trying to analyze why, she gently carried Jeremy back to the crib. He moved suddenly as her arms left him, and awakened, looking up at her as though startled. His hands reached up to clutch her hair as she bent down.

She lowered the rail so that she could kiss him and murmur soothingly, "Hush'a'bye little baby, go to sleep ... sleepy town ... Mama loves, Mama loves baby ..."

His eyes closed again and his fingers loosened on her hair and fell back to rest against his cheeks. But when she finally turned away and quietly drew up the side rail of the crib and went just as quietly toward the bedroom, his eyes opened and cut slowly sideways to watch her leave the room. He stared at the blank rectangle of the doorway, steadily, with no eye movement, for a very long while before he grew limp, his arms out-flung, his eyes staring blankly now.

Celta sat under the pool of her reading lamp, her hands folded in her lap. She had taken her bath and put on her long flannel nightgown and robe. And now she waited for drowsiness, for she had never been able to go to bed and lie there waiting for sleep to come.

Hours had passed as she sat waiting. The cuckoo clock in the kitchen chirped a number of times, irritatingly, interrupting the silence, either eleven or twelve times. She didn't count. Didn't think about counting until silence filled in the echo of the noise once again.

"*Celta*."

It was a faint call, from somewhere in the front of the house, beyond her own door, beyond the kitchen door. She sat forward abruptly, her heart leaping, hands gripping the arms of her chair. Felicia's.

"Yes?" she called back, loudly, as she hurried through the rooms. "What is it?"

She reached the swinging doors of the kitchen, and pushed them open to find the lower hall in darkness. Had she forgotten to turn the light on?"

"Felicia?"

Silence now, as profound as any she had ever encountered. She felt for the switches and turned on the light. Felicia was not in the hallway. Celta hurried along again, passing the closed doors to the library, the shadowed, long side hall to the east terrace. She went on toward the front stairway. Then she heard a sob, behind her, that drew her to a stop. The sob was very close, but Celta hesitated, unable to locate the room from which it had come. She called out again, "Felicia?"

"*Celta.*"

It was a quiet, anguished cry, a sob in the throat, and it was coming from the library. Celta hurried back again and opened one of the double doors. The room was totally dark, the draperies at the east window drawn tightly, closing out even the starlight. Celta moved uncertainly into the room, into the darkness, and paused, her eyes peering short-sightedly into a darkness that was all the more intense after the lighted hall.

The wall switches that turned on all the reading lamps were to her right, nestled somewhere in that darkness behind the opened door. Her step faltered. She felt a sudden dread at going farther into the dark, that room. She felt the absence of Felicia, of every living thing. There was only the smell of books, of a closed fireplace, of furniture polish. Of old wood.

"Felicia?"

"*Celta.*"

Softly, so softly, only a breath, a whisper, to her left in the deepest shadows of the large room, over by the long leather sofa, it seemed.

She moved in that direction, and saw a bluish glow, an unearthly light, faint, pale, coming from somewhere behind the sofa. She bumped against its corner. And stopped abruptly, for it was not Felicia there, but Jeremy, reaching toward her, standing alone in blue pajamas that covered him from his neck to his toes.

The smile on his face was angelic. His arms were lifting up toward her, and he was coming forward, one unsteady step after the other, while she stood frozen in horror.

Instinct for survival released her from the captivity of fear, and she clumsily flung herself around to face the door, but she had forgotten the sofa in her path. Her left thigh struck the arm and she fell, going down hard onto her stomach, her arms reaching out for the safety that lay beyond the deeply shadowed room.

She screamed, once, a long, desperate quavering cry.

FELICIA HAD BEEN SITTING NUMBLY on the edge of her bed for some time when she heard the scream. It came through the walls as from far away, a sound she had never heard before, half-human, half-animal, filled with fear and pain inexpressible through other means, and she knew instantly and terrifyingly that it was Celta. She threw the bedroom door open when she burst past it, so hard it banged against the wall and closed itself again. She ran through darkened hallways to the service stairway and kept upright only by her clutch on the handrails on each side. There was no light in the stairwell, or the hall between the stairs and the utility room. In the kitchen the light from Celta's room glowed faintly.

The house had grown quiet now, the long scream dying away, and only Felicia's pounding footsteps followed her. She didn't call out; her breath was drawn tight into her throat and chest.

Celta's rooms were empty. The bed had been turned down neatly, a triangle of blue plaid blankets uncovering a white pillow in an embroidered pillow case. The only light was the one by Celta's chair.

Felicia ran back, and through the swinging doors into the wide, carpeted lower hall. She saw the library door standing half open. She went toward it, her steps slowing and soundless on the carpet.

It was a scene of horror, to her left, on the floor at the end of the dark brown sofa. The unearthly blue light that emanated from him turned the blood that soaked Celta's garments, her hair, the carpet around her, a strange, purple-black. He lifted his head from Celta's throat as a predator would lift its head from its ravaged prey, blood dripping from his face, and from the hand that clawed toward her in fury at being disturbed. The sound from his throat was a sibilant and continuous hissing.

She backed away and he followed her, crawling over the torn and mutilated face and throat of his victim, coming toward Felicia on his hands and knees in swift little darts, the four white baby teeth exposed in a vicious snarl, the pink tongue pointed and darting and dripping blood. He was fast, faster than she had ever known he could be, covering the distance between them swiftly, almost reaching her as she continued to move backwards, unable to take her eyes from him, afraid to take her eyes from him, seeing him change form in movement as though metamorphosing to a more natural state, his lower body becoming the body of a serpent, whipping him along with incredible swiftness.

Light ... *the light*!

*Dear God, the light.*

She came up sharply against the edge of the door, gripped it in her hands and whirled, rounding it, reaching for the wall and the light switches. A sob of pure terror rose from her as she felt the tug of his hand on her jeans and the stinging whip of the tail as it encircled her ankle. Her hands raked hard down over the row of wall switches, and the lights blazed on, all of them, all over the large room.

When she turned he was gone. She was left alone with the brightly illuminated body of Celta, the blood a rich red now and already congealing in the pulpy mass that had been her face such a short time ago.

Felicia's eyes remained on Celta only a moment. Moving slowly and cautiously, casting quick glances over her shoulders right and left, searching out each recess, each shadow thrown by a piece of furniture, she worked her way slowly, slowly into the hall, to the next row of light switches, and turned them all on, so that even the huge crystal chandelier in the foyer was brilliant with light for the first time in years. At the closed door of the music room she turned the knob as slowly as she had moved, as she still moved, and threw the door wide open. With extreme caution she went forward in the path of light from the foyer to a lamp and turned it on, and then she circled the room, turning on every lamp as she went, and when she reached the switch that controlled the ceiling light she turned that on also.

*If he found the circuit box that controlled all the lights in the house ...*

She dared not think of that, of the house being plunged into total darkness in the space of a heartbeat. He would not know about the circuit box, and the power it wielded.

She climbed the stairway to the nursery and turned on the ceiling light there and forced her steps forward to the crib, her breath held, a prayer unformed. Had he returned and was he sleeping now, as a baby should sleep, in deep innocence? Assuring that lights were on behind her, around her, would be unnecessary then, for she was never safer than when she held him in her arms.

She stared at the inert form in the crib. His arms were thrown wide again as though the entering of the other world, the other being, cost a convulsive effort. His eyes gazed with the blankness of a doll's eyes. With the flatness of a serpent. At the corner of his open mouth oozed a drop of moisture. She started to reach down and wipe it away, but withdrew her hand without touching him. For a long moment she stood watching, and then she raised her head and looked toward her mother's dark rooms.

Moving slowly and cautiously again, she went through the house from hallway to hallway, room to room, turning lights on, drawing draperies and blinds against the darkness outside the window. She entered the far rooms of the west wing and lighted them, opened and lighted rooms that hadn't been opened in years.

Occasionally she went back to the nursery and found him yet in his trance, and so she knew that he remained somewhere in the dark of the house, watching for her. When no lights were left unburning in the house, anywhere, she returned to the library, taking with her a large bath towel. She went down on her knees beside the still body of Celta, and, with her face turned half away, wrapped the towel around the bloodied head. She brought a small Tabriz rug from the living room, and rolled Celta onto it. Gripping its end, she laboriously pulled her burden from the library and down the halls, into the kitchen, and finally into Celta's bedroom. Raising her onto the bed was more difficult. Her arms were weak and trembling, and she paused to sit on the floor beside Celta and sob wearily.

*Turn the lights on, Celta. Don't go into a dark room, Celta. Be careful.*

Why hadn't she told Celta? Celta would have understood about the touches in the dark of the night. Why hadn't she told her?

*Turn on the light. Don't leave me alone, Celta.*

She got to her feet and again struggled to lift Celta's body onto the bed, and succeeded finally, and laid her straight, on her back, and pulled the blue plaid blanket up over her, covering even the towel-wrapped head.

She closed the curtains and the blinds tightly, and shut the door behind her as she left.

DAWN HAD APPEARED over the land, the light of a new day glimmering through the uncovered kitchen window and turning the electric lights pale.

The maids would be arriving soon. And Clint.

Felicia took the rings of keys from the drawer where Celta kept them and locked Celta's room, and with the key ring slipped over her wrist she went back upstairs, to the nursery, to the bedroom beside the nursery.

# CHAPTER 18

She looked down upon her sleeping infant. His cheeks were rosy and warm to the touch, and he had turned onto his side and drawn his arms and legs together so that he looked like a fuzzy little blue caterpillar drawn into a ball. With a soft cry Felicia sank to her knees at the side of the crib, her forehead pressed against the cold wood slats. For several minutes she remained in that position, in a kind of wordless, faithless prayer.

A bell pealed faintly. It was the back door. She straightened, pulled herself up and composed herself. Jeremy had not moved. She tucked his blankets around him.

She went downstairs to the back door and unlocked it. Imogene and Alice stood there in their coats, waiting to get in, faces puzzled. This was most unusual. They had never found the service door locked before, had never been let into the house by anyone other than Celta. Both of them looked beyond the pale, large-eyed girl in jeans and sweater, who held on her wrist the huge collection of keys that were usually Celta's, looked beyond her for Celta and did not see her. They edged into the service hallway to stand facing Felicia.

"I won't be needing your help any longer," Felicia said in cool control. "I know this is unexpected, but after what happened yesterday evening to my friend, Gary, I won't be staying here any longer. I'll mail checks to both of you for one month's severance pay."

They each murmured their thanks and prepared to go, but with her hand on the doorknob Imogene felt obliged to ask, "How is the baby this morning?"

"He's fine, thank you." Felicia stood waiting for them to go, trying to still her growing anxiety. She knew instinctively what was coming next. She had seen their searching gazes go toward the kitchen, the utility room, the enclosed back stairway.

"Is Celta sick this morning?"

Felicia glanced over her shoulder. A portion of the kitchen was visible from here, but Celta's closed door was not. "All of this has made her feel rather tired," she said carefully. "I told her to stay in bed this morning, since I was going to start the closing of the house anyway. But she's fine, really. I'm sure she's eager to leave."

"Where's she going?"

"Probably back to Ireland."

"Oh? I thought she decided she wanted to stay here."

"Well ... since I'm closing the house ..."

*Go, please go. I can't stand here any longer. My head feels ... odd ...*

"I'll mail you your checks," she finished faintly. They nodded and moved out, one after the other, and Felicia pressed against the door, shutting it, locking it, listening until she heard one car start and leave, and then another. Overall then was a February silence, no traffic along the road, no motorboat on the river, no early morning birds singing.

She hung the ring of keys over the doorknob and went back upstairs.

Jeremy was still curled under the blankets. Beyond the window rays of light slanted across the brown grass below. Soon the warming sun would enter the nursery.

She moved to the crib, drew the blankets back and picked up her sleeping son. Cradling him in her arms she went to the rocking chair and sat down, and began rocking slowly, her voice half whispering, half singing a lullaby. Her cheek lowered to rest against the top of his head. Her lips touched and lingered against his forehead. She moved him, lifting him, hoping to wake him gently. She had to know that he was here, in her arms, in the small body that she had created from her own.

Without opening his eyes he yawned widely, and the four little white teeth glowed like pearls, not stained with blood, but white, perfect, clean.

It had been a nightmare, a terrible hallucination. None of last night had happened. Celta did not lie dead, nor Gary, nor Mama, nor anyone.

"Jeremy," she said softly. "Wake up. Wake up, Jeremy."

He squeezed his eyes into a crinkle and then opened them, and seeing her smiled sweetly, and she responded and hugged him fiercely and laughed and hugged him again. She held him away and looked into his face, and the smile he gave her. One of his fists went to his mouth and he began to suck on it hungrily.

Holding him in one arm, against one hip, Felicia got a bottle of milk from the refrigerator. For several minutes she rocked, cradling him as she always had, holding the bottle as he nursed. He held it too, both of his hands on hers. He didn't seem to mind that it was cold.

She bathed and dressed him in his newest suit, a small blue and white sailor suit. She brushed his hair carefully. She examined him minutely, as though to impress her memory for eternity.

He yawned, and almost fell asleep again as she put the tiny socks and shoes on his feet, but she tickled the tender soles and he shuddered and awakened.

*Don't sleep Jeremy, don't sleep. I've got to keep you awake. I've got to know you're still here, with me.*

Then came the small snowsuit that zipped up the front. The day looked as though it would not be cold, but the river was cold, she knew. This time of year it was very cold. And she couldn't bear to think of Jeremy being cold in the water.

"Want to go for a nice walk with Mama, Jeremy?"

"Mama ..."

She stared at him for a moment. He had spoken a word, his name for her, for the first time. No. Not really the first time. There had been other times, earlier, outside her locked door in the darkness.

He was more awake now, happy, smiling, beginning to jump

eagerly in her arms as she picked him up. She adjusted the hood on his head, settled him astraddle her left hip and waistline, and went downstairs and out the front door.

She crossed the lawn, and went down the bank of the road. She paused there, looking in both directions for cars, and seeing none, crossed the road to the slope downward toward the valley. As the valley began, there was a meadow where cattle grazed, and a fence that she had to cross. She put Jeremy down, crawled under the barbed wire, then held the wire up and urged him through. On hands and knees he crawled after her, and sat up, holding his arms up toward her.

Somewhere among the trees along the riverbank a crow cawed, and then three black birds rose into the sky and sailed effortlessly upon the air. Felicia picked up Jeremy, and turned her face toward the river.

Jeremy pointed an arm upward toward the flying trio of crows and murmured a garbled message of unformed words.

"Yes," Felicia said. "See the birdies fly."

They entered the trees, and the warmth of the sun was replaced by cold, damp air and the sound of water rushing toward the Atlantic. On the bank above the water Felicia paused and stared into the muddy, swirling depths. Recent rains to the west had raised the level almost to flood stage, and small whirlpools moved erratically about, sucking at the rock on which she stood.

Jeremy pointed downward, trustingly, his soft voice only a murmur against the sound of the water, but this time Felicia did not answer him. She stared at the water, until he grew restless and began to stir and whimper.

With her free hand she pulled his face toward hers, and kissed him.

"I love you," she whispered. "I will never leave you. Whatever you are — you are mine too."

She pulled his face down against her neck, and jumped, and it was like a deep, bottomless void of rushing cold that invaded and accepted and consumed without question. In her arms her child began to fight, his arms reaching upward for air, for life. She felt him squirming against her, small knees and feet fighting to get away from her. She held him tighter now, both arms wrapped around him, and allowed the water to suck them swiftly in toward the underside of the cliff.

THE FISHERMAN HAD PARKED his truck on the dirt road that wound south of the river, had taken out the tackle box and his fiberglass fishing rod. Whistling, he walked through the trees to the riverside. There was a rather still pool that he was going to try even though the river was up and looking a bit angry. When he saw the person standing on the edge of the cliff across the river, he stopped and stared. This was unexpected. Only in the summertime was he apt to see someone on that cliff, in the summertime when the river was several feet lower and that cliff served as a diving board. His whistle drawn down to an underbreath wheeze, he saw that the person across the river was a girl and she was holding a baby in her arms. And she was standing too close to the edge. Then something flew up from brush on his right and his eyes jerked away for a moment.

When he looked back the girl was gone, the baby was gone, and the water beneath the cliff was rolling something bright and sucking it down, down and beneath that table-like protrusion of rock.

He began to run forward, then remembering his rod and box he flung them aside, and, running, began removing the items of clothing that would impede his swimming. He thought of running back to his truck, of using his C.B. to call for help, but by that time it would be too late to save them.

ONCE AGAIN THE townspeople gathered for the funeral of a member of the Marchant family, for someone they had never seen. They filed slowly past the tiny casket that rested among the funeral flowers and looked down for the first and last time into the face of a baby stilled forever. He might have died in his sleep, he was so perfect, so beautiful, so at peace. The soft blue of the quilted satin lining of his permanent resting place reflected only faintly from his translucent skin, with the merest suggestion of the violence of his death. The only member of the family present at this funeral was Mildred's husband, Leonard

Stewart, if he could be called family anymore. It was said he was the child's grandfather, and not his father at all. This was something that not even the most imaginative of the town's gossips had suspected. The mother, Felicia, was so young.

Outside on the church lawn the people gathered, having passed the coffin dutifully, and discussed this latest tragedy of Jonesboro and the Marchant family. The girl, Felicia, had been revived in the ambulance on the way to the hospital. No, it was in the hospital, my niece is a nurse, and she was there. But she came back raving, clearly out of her mind, you know. Said she killed her baby because he wasn't normal, said horrible things, that somehow he had *killed* her mother, and Gary Appleby, and Martin Marchant, and old Celta. But of course that was nonsense. Celta McDowell was not even dead. She had already gone back to Ireland.

The whole thing was ridiculous. Poor Felicia.

It was the shock, the doctor told me. First, the shock of the other deaths, and finally, the shock of her baby's death.

Poor girl.

Her father is taking her away, you know, as soon as the funeral is over. My niece says she's able to travel, and she's stopped raving and just walks around the hospital room or stares out the window. The doctors told Leonard Stewart she'll be all right once she gets a few months of California sunshine. Johnny Bishop out at the airport says there's a private plane standing by and ready to leave as soon as the baby is laid away in the family crypt.

What's going to happen to Tanglewood now?

Clint Reilly will see after it. He's got a lifetime job there, he said. Twice a year he's supposed to open the house and have it cleaned. And he'll keep the grounds in order.

Well, Clint's got more nerve than most of us. I wouldn't go out there and work around the edge of those woods for anything.

# OTHER NOVELS BY RUBY JEAN

1974 *The House that Samael Built*
1974 *Seventh All Hallows' Eve*
1974 *House at River's Bend*
1975 *The Girl Who Didn't Die*
1978 *Child of Satan's House*
1978 *Satan's Sister*
1978 *Dark Angel*
1982 *Hear the Children Cry*
1982 *Such a Good Baby*
1983 *The Lake*
1983 *MaMa*
1985 *Home Sweet Home*
1985 *Best Friends*
1986 *Wait and See*
1987 *Annabelle*
1987 *Chain Letter*
1988 *Smoke*
1988 *House of Illusions*
1988 *Jump Rope*

## OTHER NOVELS BY RUBY JEAN

*1989 Pendulum*
*1989 Death Stone*
*1990 Vampire Child*
*1990 Lost and Found*
*1990 Victoria*
*1991 Celia*
*1991 Baby Dolly*
*1992 The Reckoning*
*1993 The Living Evil*
*1994 The Haunting*
*1995 Night Thunder*
*2022 Bear Hollow Charlie*
*2022 Cry of the Soul*
*2022 Pride of Bella Terra*

www.ingramcontent.com/pod-product-compliance
Lightning Source LLC
Chambersburg PA
CBHW060558310726
48982CB00008B/1162/J